Literature and the Internet
A Guide for Students, Teachers, and Scholars

Stephanie Browner, Stephen Pulsford, and Richard Sears

Garland Publishing, Inc.
A member of the Taylor & Francis Group
New York & London
2000

Learning Resources
Centre
/ 2 43292 ✗

Published in 2000 by
Garland Publishing, Inc.
A member of the Taylor & Francis Group
19 Union Square West
New York, NY 10003

10 9 8 7 6 5 4 3 2 1

Library of Congress Cataloging-in-Publication Data

Browner, Stephanie.
    Literature and the Internet : a guide for students, teachers, and
scholars / Stephanie Browner, Richard Sears, Stephen Pulsford.
        p.   cm. — (Wellesley studies in critical theory, literary
history, and culture ; v. 21. Garland reference library of the
humanities ; v. 2167)
    Includes bibliographical references (p.) and index.
    ISBN 0-8153-3453-2
    1. Literature—Research—Computer network resources.   I. Sears,
Richard.   II. Pulsford, Stephen.   III. Title.   IV. Series: Garland
reference library of the humanities. Wellesley studies in critical
theory, literary history, and culture ; vol. 21.   V. Series: Garland
reference library of the humanities ; vol. 2167.
PN73.B76   1999
802′.85—dc21   99-27760
                                                                  CIP

Printed on acid-free, 250-year-life paper.
Manufactured in the United States of America

Contents

Introduction

The Internet, even in such a relatively limited field as literature, is too multi-faceted to be grasped, too broad to be covered by any one writer, or even by any three. In this particular instance, all three of us are aware that we have left many nooks and crannies of our subject matter unexplored. Nevertheless, our collaboration has produced a text representing several points of view, approaching the Internet and literature from at least three distinct perspectives, and, at least in that sense, covering a very wide spectrum.

Part I, by Richard Sears, composed of Chapters 1 through 5, takes a general, practical stance, addressing, for the most part, ordinary readers and students who want some direction in exploring Internet literary sites. Understanding Part I does not require a degree, or even a major, in English or special training in computer technology and software. This part deals most consciously with the actual experience of using the Internet and is neither particularly academic nor especially theoretical.

Part II, by Stephanie Browner (Chapters 6 through 8) is more academic, focusing on the educational concerns of students, teachers, and literary scholars. Chapter 6 deals with pedagogical issues such as plagiarism, citation, and website evaluation, whereas Chapter 7 surveys how English teachers use the Internet in literature courses. Chapter 8, the most technical chapter, describes how electronic texts are created and discusses the scholarly and professional issues raised by the advent of the Internet.

Part III, by Stephen Pulsford (Chapter 9) is theoretical, although this part, like the others, avoids jargon and, unlike many contemporary analyses (of any intellectual subject), seeks to clarify rather than obfuscate the issues. The writer lays out the problems, deals with them in an orderly, lucid fashion, and then moves on. This part deals with the cultural implications of the Internet and literature.

It is possible, and perhaps profitable, to read the whole book all the way through, but readers with limited time may want to turn directly to the part that best suits their needs. We have tried to provide a variety of instructions, descriptions, definitions, analyses, and opinions. For those who wish to avoid all that content, the large, annotated bibliography of Internet sources, complete with addresses (URLs) for each site, may prove to be the most valuable part of the book. Any user—even the rawest novice—can visit hundreds of literary home pages without benefit of anyone else's ideas, advice, or theorizing.

After all, our primary desire as writers of this guide to literature and the Internet is to promote and enable individual exploration. Each reader must choose his or her own path through our book and through the Internet itself.

Acknowledgments

We would like to thank Sandy Bolster and Rebecca Bates for comments on earlier versions, the Appalachian College Association and Berea College for financial support, Berea College librarians for their assistance, and student researchers Ivan Svetlicec and Oana Sirboiu for their contribution to the list of sites.

CHAPTER 1

The Internet as a Whole

WHY?

For people who are primarily interested in literature, reading books about the Internet may seem pointless. Many guides to cyberspace list jargon and instructions about how to perform operations most readers would never want to perform. A few purport to serve only the interests of the dim-witted. One Internet text, *Using the Internet: The Most Complete Reference*, which is extra long but otherwise typical in many respects, has well over a thousand pages of definitions and functions, but nothing in the entire work suggests why anyone should wish to use the web in the first place or details what resources are actually available via Internet. Reading books about the Internet is generally not encouraging for those more interested in an academic discipline than in computers.

A quick look at the Internet itself scarcely motivates scholarly exploration, since its immediate appearance evokes billboards, television, and video games. This impression is not a false one: The Internet displays tons of material that is commercial, colorful, entertaining, and interactive, as well as occasionally loud and intrusive.

In addition, even a short journey through the World Wide Web indicates that the Internet is incredibly vast and daunting. The net is so large that many recent accounts simply explain why its size cannot be accurately established, and some critics have claimed that looking for information on the Internet is like trying to drink from a firehose. Why should a serious-minded scholar or reader waste precious time exploring a frustrating, overloaded virtual universe of advertising, hype, doubtful amusement, and trivia?

The answers are so simple that they may seem uncompelling:

1. The Internet is an enormous, in some ways unique, academic resource. In many important respects, the Internet is a new kind of library, an

electronic library of libraries, with text, pages, books, collections of books, and collections of collections.

2. The Internet is immediately accessible, quite easy to search, and easier to use than the typical university library. For some kinds of information, the Internet is much the quickest route; for other kinds, which are on the increase, the Internet is the only source available.

TEXT

The material of the Internet is mostly text, divided into pages. In fact, the page (as in *home page,* for example) is the basic unit of Internet sites, which are produced with software closely related to or identical with word processors. Ordinarily, a whole lot of words on pages collected together would clearly appear to us as books. Only the necessity of viewing the assembled words on computer screens prevents our seeing the leaflets, pamphlets, magazines, and books that readers *usually* read and literary scholars habitually dealt with long before computers existed. For people whose occupations or majors include the study of literature, the Internet is an extension of their ordinary interests into a new realm, but text on the Internet is still text, even though it is not between cardboard covers.

There are differences between books and Internet pages, of course, but not necessarily the ones we have been led to expect. For example, some writers have stated that Internet text is delivered in the form of sound bites, little television commercial–sized portions, but although such units may be found, one is just as likely to turn up enormous files: All Shakespeare's plays are on the Internet, and none of them is geared toward the hypothetical short attention span of computer users; all *The Iliad*, all *The Odyssey*, all *The Divine Comedy* appear on the Internet also. Since much of the text on the Internet is derived from the textual forms in the "real" world, much of it is simply the size of its inspiration.

The four primary differences between text on the Internet and text in actual books are that Internet texts are searchable, connected, collectible, and reproducible. The first two capacities permit the reader to study and relate to texts in new, solely electronic modes, whereas the last two primarily give the reader new powers of manipulating and possessing texts in print.

1. Internet text is searchable, not simply because it appears on the Internet but also because it appears in relationship to the word functions of computers. All word processors have search capacities; all web browsers have search capacities; and absolutely all the texts one may discover at Internet sites can be searched, sometimes in multiple ways. Word-by-word textual analysis, which used to depend on concordances laboriously compiled for only a very few works (the Bible and Shakespeare), is now possible for an

enormous range of literary works and is available to anyone, academic scholar or not. Techniques for style identification via computer (using not just big, important words, but *the, and, but,* and so on) have been developed by linguists and are being used now; the identifying differences between the styles of (say) John Steinbeck and Jane Austen can be numerically defined and demonstrated. Whether or not Shakespeare wrote a particular work is a different kind of question than it used to be since the subtlest discriminations of usage can be compiled and scrutinized. In addition, the Internet, of course, makes thousands of texts available for such *scientific* study.

2. Internet text routinely connects to other texts, and any Internet site has the potential to connect to any other site. The World Wide Web is called a web because it is interconnected to itself at point after point. From any site on the Internet, a link can be made that enables the user to move directly and immediately to any other site, a physical impossibility for even the most agile of real-world spiders. This "any point to any point" feature depends completely on the use of hypertext on the Internet, so the connections (or links, as they are called) are the basic differentiation of text on the Internet from text anywhere else. Other text forms may be searchable, collectible, and reproducible in some way, but they are not linked. Because of the linking, virtually all Internet sites appear in a matrix of other sites. Whether or not coherence is perceivable on a local level (why is that particular site attached to this one?), the total impression is of a vast coinherence of knowledge. Never has literature seemed so "related" to all the other concerns of the human race.

3. Internet text is collectible in a very immediate way, since most sites allow files to be downloaded and used like any other computer files. Usually, downloading a file is possible in two different modes: as a text file or as a source file. A text file eliminates the images from a site and provides only the words, which can then be manipulated as in any other word-processing file. If a person wants to insert annotations into a complete text of *Hamlet,* for example, it is possible to do so; in fact, once it becomes a text file, any work of literature can be altered in any way. A source file stores all the information of the original site in hypertext markup language (HTML) so that it can be opened and used on the user's computer; in this format, it looks exactly as it did on the Internet, and although it can also be changed, the process is rather difficult and thus not very likely.

4. Internet text can be reproduced electronically (copied and recopied, cut and pasted here, there, and everywhere) or it can be printed as hard copy. Most files can be printed directly from the Internet browser (Netscape or Microsoft Explorer, for example), and, of course, any text that can be downloaded as the user's own file can be printed in the ordinary way. Thus, a

student who needs to read Chapter 1 of *Pride and Prejudice* can easily print a copy of her own from an e-text version. Actually purchasing certain kinds of textbooks may very well become obsolete.

The changes that the Internet may bring about in our use of literature have not yet developed clearly, but it seems reasonable to predict that the four differentiae mentioned above contribute to several new emphases in literary studies: the possibility of more scientific approaches to texts, a new sense of interrelatedness between texts and texts and between texts and the world; a new capacity for flexibility and change within the text itself, and the reader's altered style of text "ownership."

INTERNET LIBRARY (PRIMARY TEXTS)

Conceiving of the Internet as a vast library is enticing for literary scholars; it makes a brave new world seem accessible and manageable on old, familiar terms. It must be acknowledged, however, that the Internet is composed of a whole new breed of text collection, in many crucial respects unlike any other library on earth.

To characterize the primary texts, actual literary works, represented on the net, one must draw analogies to bookstores as well as libraries. A reader at the Internet, so to speak, can readily find works that would otherwise appear in specialized archives, graduate school libraries, rare book collections, antiquarian bookstores, airport terminal stalls, discount chains, adult bookstores, sidewalk newsstands, small-town public libraries, and floor-to-ceiling used bookstores, to name a few. All these sources of books appear on the same level, and all are acessible through the same means: the most democratic, variegated, surprising lot of books ever assembled in one—let us say—realm.

Among the works on the Internet that would ordinarily be published some other way, however, one seldom encounters the current books that are appearing in mainstream bookstores right now. Copyright restrictions prevent Internet publication of recent titles. Biographical information about the most current writers, advertisements for their titles, and the most up-to-date reviews are all easy to find, but not the books that Barnes and Noble stocks by the thousands. For that reason, the Internet "library" collection has a strange twist: It has large and obvious gaps, it cannot cover the literary ground as even a moderately well-stocked library can, and it cannot equal the contemporary appeal of a good bookstore.

The library of the Internet, however, contains sources that are almost inaccessible through any other collection. Among these are hypertext publications of archival rarities such as slave narratives or eighteenth-century fiction by little-known female writers. Texts that would be prohibitive as reprint editions appear on the Internet—more and more frequently—at low cost compared with traditional publishing methods. Hundreds, perhaps thousands, of texts that would once have been very difficult to access are now at the scholar's fingertips.

Still other Internet resources are really not available *anywhere* else, including journals published only in electronic editions and fiction and poetry composed in hypertext in the first place. In addition to those works, which are structurally tied into the Internet, a host of writings appear in cyperspace simply because it is an available place for publication. Letters, diaries, commentaries, reflections, sexual confessions, diatribes, poetry, essays, short stories, and novels from the pens of people whose works less than a decade ago would never have been published are now occupying shelf space on the net, and only on the net. Walt Whitman's egalitarian crowds, some uttering barbaric yawps, have found their niche.

RESEARCH LIBRARY

Because the vast majority of literary works published since the 1920s cannot be displayed on the Internet, secondary texts relating to literary works and authors far outnumber primary ones on the net. Every sort of encyclopedic reference appears on the web. Some sites feature literally thousands of entries of a biographical or historical slant, and it is safe to say that every past author we have ever heard of is discussed somewhere on the Internet. Many electronic encyclopedias contain only materials readily available in any ordinary reference collection, but they all have the advantage of links to facilitate their cross references. All other things being equal, an Internet encyclopedia is a bit more efficient to use than the same set in print and between covers.

Some biographical (and autobiographical) and journalistic information on the Internet is more current than the data in any library, simply because Internet sites may be updated weekly or even daily. The most famous newspapers in the world—and TV news channels, weather channels, shopping channels, arts channels, and film channels—have Internet versions of their stories and schedules, provided every day and frequently available before any other form of report. The Internet is an invaluable pop culture treasure trove, and since book publishers strive to keep up with all the other media, the most contemporary, up-to-date literary *news* is on the Internet.

Of more interest (perhaps) to the academic user is that the Internet has become the repository for home pages of the most respected intellectual institutions in the world, including, of course, virtually all the major colleges and universities; all the major libraries and archives, including, in the United States alone, the Library of Congress, the National Archives, all the state historical societies, the National Geographic Society, the Smithsonian; and virtually all the major art museums, opera houses, and theaters. These home pages contain valuable links to other sources chosen by the (generally) well-informed staffs of these major institutions. In short, the Internet is an unparalleled cultural treasure trove, too.

UNLIKENESS TO LIBRARIES

The Internet offers literary texts and primary and secondary resources arranged in pages like the books that websites have copied so quickly. Although it would seem that the experience of reading literature on the Internet would be much the same as any previous way of reading, it is not.

The Internet as a library, for example, exhibits some very peculiar features. It is a huge collection of textual sites, but site after site offers nothing beyond what is already available on hundreds of other sites; these duplicates may even be linked to each other, so that the unwary reader may be invited to move from clone to clone to clone on a trail set up by the clone makers. Very frequently, in fact, materials are connected and totally redundant (whereas when reading a book, turning the page to find the same page would not be permissible!). It begins to seem as if there are a thousand versions of the same thing. Just visit any list of a thousand Shakespeare sites for ready examples. Please note that *AltaVista* reports 503,430 Shakespeare sites on the Internet!

Of course, it is sometimes convenient to have many different routes to the same place, but it can also be confusing and time consuming. Often, the Internet is like being in a big city where all the streets look alike and you are trying to locate only one of them.

In actual libraries, such a configuration is rare, since publishers generally avoid simple duplications of previously published works and collection builders consciously avoid collecting all the same books again. At present, there is no sense on the Internet of gaps being filled or missing areas of information being supplied; there is no sense whatever of a total vision of the realm of knowledge. Perhaps such a vision is now out of the question.

OUT OF DATE ALREADY

A major difference between the virtual library of the web and the "real" world of libraries is that the Internet is (more) frequently redundant; another major difference is that the Internet is frequently outdated. In fact, the Internet tends to *begin* with the outdated! The web certainly looks au courant with bright, attractive colors, an ultracontemporary context, and immediate accessibility, but appearances can be deceiving.

In literature home pages, the Internet occasionally seems outmoded, both in theory and in content. At a time when postmodernism minimizes categories and hierarchies, the web reinstates and emphasizes them. The easiest way to present information on the Internet—by now, the traditional way—is in nested hierarchies; everything has a category that fits under another category and so on. The subject tree format is everywhere on the web. Postmodern assumptions about equality of texts and blurring of boundaries within genres and between periods have no place in the formal arrangements of web pages.

The commonest designation for a website is simply an author's name. By default, the Internet perpetuates a completely auteuristic theory of literarature. So much attention is given to individual authors that larger issues of literary history, criticism, and theory receive very little notice; such subjects are given much less attention in virtual libraries than in real ones. To a certain extent, the *shape* of the net alters theories of literary study. Form becomes meaning.

THE OLD CANON

Old versions of the literary canon reign supreme on the Internet, even though sideshows about women and ethnic groups accompany the main carnival. Or rather, old canons reign supreme with a slight but meaningful distinction. Authors whose work is out of copyright command more space and attention than those whose works are still under copyright. To some extent, a couple of generations of modern writers are excluded. Modernism by this accounting is much less significant than medievalism.

Every once in a while, a site announces that it is displaying copyrighted material and the site author begs not be sued, offering to remove the illegal texts instantly if anyone objects. In one case, an *e.e. cummings home page,* the site author apologizes for a basically empty page since the poems that originally appeared there were forcibly removed by the E. E. Cummings Copyright Trust.

E-texts of older authors' works tend to be copies of texts no longer under copyright, so more recent, perhaps more scholarly and accurate, editions are seldom used. Many e-text archives represent academic steps backward. Why read the authoritative, expensive 1997 edition in print when the unreliable, free one from 1902 is readily available on the net?

Actually, most Internet sites have had a preexistence in print, some so long ago that they seem to be ghostly visitors from the distant past, or—less romantically—dusty dissertations from some professor's bottom desk drawer. When people began to realize the potential of the Internet, they zipped onto web pages with material already in hand, myriads of it, myriads of them. Naturally, some of the material was too old to be useful, and virtually all of it was already hanging around somewhere else. Thus, the overgeneralization that the Internet began by instantly rendering itself outdated.

Yes, the Internet is very current in many, but certainly not all, respects. In a few years, it may no longer be thought necessary to fill the immensity of cyberspace with publications from the other world. In fact, it seems quite likely that the Internet will generate more and more of its own texts, in literature as in everything else. But that time has not yet come.

UNLIKENESS TO BOOKS

A reader holds a book, and almost unconsciously she makes judgments about it. She knows how large it is and how heavy. How long is it? She can look at the end to see how many pages are included. The author's name is right there on the spine; the copyright date is in the usual place. She can check the chapter titles if she wishes to get a general idea of the subject matter, and she can look at the index to see if specific people or places are mentioned. She can (probably very accurately) determine a great deal about the book's reliability, range, subject matter, and provenance without ever reading it.

Some culture critics have been writing about how important it is to be able to read books anywhere, in bed or in the bathtub. They attack computers for not being books, not being portable to the same extent, not being personal in the same way. These sentiments fail to move me, but I believe that the *estimations* we can form of books from the physical objects themselves are crucial.

The user clicks on a website and arrives. Who is the author of this rather attractive spread on Chaucer? Who knows? The author's name may or may not appear at the bottom of some page or other (not necessarily this one). Or there may be no author within the website framework: the author may have published this material decades ago in a book that the present site does not mention. Where is the date? Find it, if you can, and then interpret it. Is it the date of the publication of the text, the date the website was approved, or the date of the last time the site was updated? Or some other date? Who or what is the publisher or, more likely, the sponsoring institution? Find out, if you can. Is there a table of contents? Find it, if you can. An index? There could be. Find it, if you can. Sources? And so on.

All the old, reliable aspects of a scholarly book (or any kind of book) are displaced or missing, dropped without notice, or included, but where? These are serious derelictions for a serious reader; for a literary scholar, they may create insuperable difficulties.

Internet sites are delivered a screenful at a time. Each screen may copy a page, but the context is never as clear as the context provided by an actual book or manuscript. In my writing with a word processor, I have found that I cannot grasp a whole essay of my own composition if it is only displayed as text on a computer screen; I have to print it out to comprehend it.

The computer screen in itself is a small glimpse into potentially vast worlds. But the possible size of what the computers may display should never be confounded with the size of the user's vision of it, a vision that is perpetually limited no matter what the user is looking at, because a window is always just a window.

The conditions of use for a website and a book, even when the two contain exactly the same text, are substantially different and are likely to remain so.

I am aware that in this chapter I seem to be contradicting myself. The Internet, I claim, is something new and wonderful, or the Internet is stale and redundant. Electronic text is like any other text; electronic text is fundamentally different from any other text. An Internet site is like a book; no, it is not like a book. And so on.

Contradictions (or seeming contradictions) make up a large part of the characteristic patterns of the Internet. Art and business intermingle bizarrely, and hyperentertainment and dry statistics show up side by side. The contradictions simply exist. For that reason, among others, the Internet presents both unique opportunities and unique problems. The opportunity versus problem issue that concerns us most is how to find what we want in the midst of it all. Grasping the whole thing is almost out of the question, but using it effectively is not.

CHAPTER 2

Searching the Internet

1. BROWSERS

How Much to Learn?

How much technological expertise does an English teacher, student, or scholar need to use the Internet effectively in relationship to literature? The answer really is almost none. Of course, certain leaders in the construction, manipulation, and exploration of the web (such as computer specialists and librarians) would make other claims. Sometimes computer specialists remind me of (hypothetical) mechanics insisting that we learn the names of all automobile parts before starting on a journey, whereas librarians who have pronounced on the subject of Internet searching seem to want us to pack for all seasons before undertaking a short trip to the nearest big city.

The best way to learn how to use any of the Internet browsers, subject trees, or search engines—which are all designed to help us find what we want on the net—is simply to start using them. I will offer some advice about how to do that, without giving specific details about operations because that would be pointless. If I gave detailed instructions about how to use the browser on my computer, it would simply be misleading, for reasons that should be obvious.

The two best known, most widely used browsers are Netscape Navigator and Microsoft's Explorer (both embroiled in a recent, well-publicized court case about net dominance). Most of my examples will be drawn from Netscape, because that is the browser I use. Although it has been in existence for only a short time, Netscape already exists in several different versions. Computer software, like textbooks, always demonstrates planned obsolescence: Just as you learn it, get used to it, and even grow fond of it, the manufacturers bring out a new version, not quite compatible with some earlier versions. The older versions then have to be abandoned, although they were perfectly good, all in the name of keeping up. The result—as one moves from the computer lab to the computer at home to the computer in the library to the computer in the neighboring town—is that one is faced with many different versions of the Internet browser.

The differences between editions of Netscape are frequently only matters of terminology, not of function. For that reason, what the user needs to learn is the general *expectations* to bring to any particular browser in a specific computer system. What should Netscape do? Once expectations are formed it is relatively simple to look for the techniques that have to be learned to enable one to use a new version of the same old thing.

The first step with any browser, itself a tool for exploration, is to explore it. Probably everyone should know one version of an Internet browser very well, because the knowledge is widely applicable. Examine all the buttons, links, and pull-down screens, and familiarize yourself with the terminology. Try everything out; if you are really new to the Internet, try *literally* everything, including the links to Business, Entertainment, Sports, News, and so forth. The first time you use the Internet you should surf; but as far as I'm concerned, it is a waste of time ever to surf again, because it is almost exactly like walking around a huge shopping mall for hours although you don't want to buy anything (surfing produces the same half-intoxicated, half-stultified combination of aimlessness, guilty pleasure, and fatigue). Move from link to link to link, explore without anything in mind. Go all over the place and get lost. Then press the Home button, go back where you started, and look for the online tutorial, since almost all software of any complexity contains instructions for all the operations it performs (computers are endlessly self-referential). Online instruction is an obvious necessity since no one could carry all the required booklets from computer to computer. All you need to know will be part of the program you want to learn to use.

It is important to remember that if your primary interest is literature, not computers, you only need to learn enough computer expertise to accomplish what you want to do and to find what you want to find; everything else (and there is a lot of it)—all the jargon, the terminology, the endless technical explanations—is irrelevant. Your destination is infinitely more important than the naming of parts or packing for winter on a summer vacation.

Expectations of a Browser

At least nine important functions are part of a browser's capacities; any user should expect to find these functions in some guise on any version of Netscape or Microsoft's Explorer.

1. **Searching.** Netscape provides easy access to a variety of search engines, including one that is simply part of its own program. A small number of well-known search engines (*Lycos, Excite, Thunderstone,*

AltaVista, and others) can be reached by a single click, whereas *all* the remaining engines (with the exception of subscription services like *Ferret*) can be located by using their uniform resource locators (URLs) or by searching for them with the available search engines. (Yes, you use the search engines you have to find all the ones you don't have!)

2. **Accessing.** Accessing a site is possible in several different ways. Netscape provides an address box where the user can insert a URL to go directly to the site. Some early versions of Netscape allow access through URLs in a couple of different ways; later versions are more streamlined. In any case, only one address method is needed, since there are three other ways of accessing. Sites can also be reached by search engines, as mentioned above, by connecting links, or by bookmarks (or "favorites," as they are called in Explorer). Bookmarks are URLs plus other site data that the browser retains on command.

3. **Opening.** It is no benefit to find a file unless it can be opened and used. Netscape allows the user to access and open old-fashioned file transfer protocol (FTP) and gopher files, news groups, and other variations as well as the standard WWW (World Wide Web) sites.

4. **Displaying.** Probably the chief function of any browser is the display. Netscape enables the user to view HTML files as individual pages with text and images on a monitor screen. Those who remember what Internet displays used to look like before Mosaic, Netscape, and Explorer will realize what an incredible advance the browser is. "Now instead of entering obscure instructions by key board and staring at screens full of monotone type, users [are] able to steer through a universe of words, images, and sounds with the click of a mouse button" (Simon 39, 40). It is, in other words, *quite* a display.

5. **Remembering.** Most browsers have a feature to enable the user to keep records of sites she wishes to visit again. *Bookmarking* is the Netscape term for this capacity, and it is, by any measure, one of the most significant functions of Internet research; managing bookmarks is an important skill that is discussed in a later section. Another mode of recall is the address list where special e-mail addresses can be stored. Making bookmarks and storing e-mail addresses are decisions and actions of the user; neither will happen automatically. Netscape performs other memory functions by default, whether the user wants them done or not: the history function displays—for review or revisiting—the titles of all sites visited during a particular Netscape session. Another function, not so visible to the user, is Netscape's practice of making caches: stored copies of the files the user visits on the web that can be accessed from one's own computer, a much faster process than accessing from the Internet. (Both the his-

tory function and caching are under the control of user preferences and can be easily changed from their default settings.)

6. **Tracking.** Frequently, it is necessary to retrace one's steps on a computer journey, but for a long or complex session on the Internet, that would be impossible without some method of marking a trail. The same applies to past sessions; if you want to retrace the steps you took in a session a week ago, stored tracking is imperative. For researchers, tracking is a very important function, but even casual surfers may also find it useful. Netscape allows the user to see where he has been through the simple device of changing the color of all links that have been clicked. If you've been there, the link is purple (maybe, although it could be any color as long as it is different from the original), and if you have not been there, it is still dark blue (maybe).

7. **Downloading.** With Netscape, it is possible for a site stored on a server far away to be made part of one's own local collection of files. Then it suddenly has a life outside Netscape, a life off the Internet. The downloaded file is liable to any of the operations that a word processor can perform on a file: saving; storing; copying; changing from one type of file to another; being searched within the word-processing program; being edited, deleted, printed, or e-mailed; and so on. Plagiarism has never before been so easy, but that is the subject of a later section.

8. **Printing.** Netscape prints files on its own steam, too. Any current page (the one you see on your monitor during a Netscape session) can be printed in several different modes, including one that looks exactly like what is displayed on the computer screen (subject to having a sufficiently sophisticated color printer, of course), a version that is simply text, or a version that shows all the HTML markups.

9. **Searching.** A distinct search mechanism on Netscape (not a search engine to look for other sites) enables the user to search the page she happens to be visiting, whether or not the page itself offers the option on site. Thus, any page opened by Netscape and displayed on the screen is searchable. Any page one visits is searchable. The whole of the World Wide Web is searchable, page by page.

A Note on Gopher, Telnet, and FTP Sites

Many users whose experience of the World Wide Web predate Netscape and the other browsers may remember a rather cumbersome process involving Gophers with Veronica and Archie searchers. Gopher sites still exist, some completely unchanged, but they are now accessible via Netscape. Anyone who wants may visit a site <gopher://liberty.uc.wlu.edu/70/11/gophers/other>

where *all the gophers in the world by subject and country* are available or one called *Gopher Jewels* <http://galaxy.einet.GJ.index.html> that offers some assessment and overview. The current importance of gopher sites is certainly not what it used to be, but these sites retain some significance in relation to library catalogs and random text collections.

Most of the major libraries around the world have their catalogs available on line. Gopher sites allow the user to zero in on a particular region of the world (Venezuela, for example) and determine what libraries and other institutions there have archives and collections on electronic display.

The literary texts available through gopher searching are usually not hypertext (not linked to anything) but are just word-processing files of some sort, although they are relatively easy to download and may be useful upon occasion. For example, when I was editing a text of *Volpone* for production, I found a gopher file of the folio edition that I used as a basis for my version without the necessity of typing any of it. Still, so much material is now available on the Internet that gopher technology seems mostly obsolete.

FTP files designed for transfer from one computer to another are almost completely nonliterary now, although some texts were accessible in that mode a few years ago. They may not have disappeared altogether, but I could not locate any that were even minimally interesting.

Telnet links are included in some websites, and Netscape's most recent versions support Telnet sessions, displaying a separate window for the process. Telnet sites, such as library catalogs mentioned above, play by their own rules, however. Generally, Netscape can bring the user to the entry point of a Telnet site, where login and a password may be required (sometimes a Netscape site provides the requisite information, password and all). After entering, the user must conform to the rules and procedures within the site, and he must go out as he came in; within a typical Telnet site there are no external links to the web, so activity within it is self-contained.

Bookmarking

The most efficient method of bookmarking—particularly while exploring a delimited subject, in this case literature, on the net—is *not* saving an entry for every interesting site one visits. Bookmarking every site one might want to revisit results in a cumbersome, unsorted list of hundreds of sites, including many with titles that convey absolutely nothing about their content (such as *CWIS Listings, Republic of Pemberley, The Mining Co., EDSITEment, Bibliomania,* and *AHDS Homepage*). Of course, a collector of literary bookmarks might choose only sites named for periods, genres, and authors, but such a familiar proliferation would still become very unwieldy and basically unhelpful.

The best approach to bookmarking is to focus on links pages. Bookmarking the links pages instead of the sites with actual content may seem wrong-headed, rather like reading only tables of contents. The best subject tree sites, such as *The Voice of the Shuttle* or Jack Lynch's *Online Literary Research,* however, offer links to hundreds of other sites, sorted into categories so that they can be easily located. One link to a site such as *Internet Sites for Choice Magazine* or, for that matter, to my own *Departmental Guide to the Internet: A Webliography* is the equivalent of bookmarking every item on an enormous, selected, annotated list of literary links.

One may decide to bookmark links pages that run the gamut from the most general coverage (every kind of topic, including the academic) through the academic only, through literary sites only, through period sites only, to the most specific (links pages for individual authors). Such focused links pages as "The Jane Austen Information Page" on the *Republic of Permberley* site or the "Best.sites" page on *Mr. Shakespeare and the Internet* also access dozens or even hundreds of sites within one or two clicks.

All this is not to deny that literary users will find websites so beautiful and useful, so visitable, that bookmarking them is imperative, but the most sensible general practice is still bookmarking the links.

Annotating Bookmarks

Most browsers provide techniques for annotating bookmarks, a very useful practice for long lists or for webliographies designed for research or publication. One's bookmarks may very well and very easily become a large part of one's home page, for example, or part of a course site. Unfortunately, the annotation function varies from edition to edition of Netscape and is altogether absent from Internet Explorer. (I could not be sure about the last matter without consulting a complete handbook for Explorer. I approached the browser with the *expectation* that it would allow me to annotate bookmarks, but I could not locate such a function; a lab technician assured me that the function does not exist.)

The Netscape variations are an excellent instance of how different editions of the same software change terminology a great deal and actual techniques very little. Netscape Navigator 2.01 provides a very simple approach: The user opens a bookmarks window, clicks on edit, and has immediate access to a box where an annotation can be inserted. Netscape 3.0 adds another step, whereas in Netscape Navigator 4.04 the user opens a bookmark window, clicks on edit, and then chooses an option called "Bookmark Properties" that opens another window where clicking on edit opens a box in which an annotation may be written. (This brief technical tale should have a cautionary effect; the easiest and most efficient version of this important function is the earliest.)

Of course, a bookmarks file that has been converted into a word-processing file (a somewhat laborious business, if you ask me) can then have annotations or anything else added or edited, but that eliminates the possibility of displaying annotated bookmarks within Netscape itself and eliminates the possibility of using annotations within the Internet working environment.

2. SEARCHING THE INTERNET

Two Basic Search Approaches

Searching the Internet effectively can be approached in two radically different ways: through general access (from the top down) or through specific access (from the bottom up). For most subjects of inquiry both techniques are needed, since neither by itself yields full results and each by itself has built-in, unavoidable problems. Some researchers use only one, usually the specific access technique, to the detriment of their research. Incidentally, it is common for a particular site, literary or otherwise, to offer a subject tree of its own and a search facility of its own as well. The two frequently appear together within sites.

General access searching involves subject trees and subject guides (both discussed below), such as *The Voice of the Shuttle (VOS), Yahoo!,* and *Magellan, Online Literary Resources.* The concept of the subject tree is simple: Begin with big general categories and gradually focus on more specific categories. A typical hierarchy from *VOS* runs Literature (English): American: Nineteenth Century: Louisa May Alcott: *Behind a Mask: or, A Woman's Power,* a complete e-text provided by the University of Virginia Library, with other Alcott works also represented at this level. For any specific period or author, it is possible to approach the subject from the top, so to speak. One possible advantage of this method is simply that the site has already been consciously chosen by someone on some basis or other, which may indicate that it possesses a distinction of some sort. Another advantage of this method is that it may help the user to know the provenance of the page once it has been reached. General access searching tends to make context easier to discern. This page is part of that site which is part of that organization's territory and so on.

On the other hand, the bottom-up method makes context very difficult (sometimes impossible) to ferret out. Specific access searching involves the use of search engines (discussed below), such as *AltaVista, Lycos, Metacrawler Searching,* and *Dogpile.* Typically, search engines are used to find some very specific name or title. The results of a search engine session (called hits) arrive on the page with little truncated descriptions, and when the user visits a hit, he may very well find himself on a dead-end page, linked to nothing, not even the home page, or on a page that supples no information about itself. It may be very difficult to locate or reconstruct a context for a particular site located by a search engine.

The primary problem of the top down method is rather different. Here, the issue of coverage is most crucial. When traveling down a list of categories in a subject tree, the user may arrive at the place where Eudora Welty might be expected only to discover she is not included at all. Only with repeated use and practice will the user know what to expect to find in a particular subject tree, but she will never know if the subject tree is including the best, a sampling, or every instance of a given subject. Only prolonged searching using several different types of search engines can provide that information.

With a subject tree search, one is faced with the task of moving through various categories and subcategories, whereas with a search engine search, one is faced with the sometimes overwhelming chore of selecting from a huge list of apparently random hits, with each hit an individual, unrelated thing. Search engines have some real advantages, but clarifying the context of an individual site is not one of them.

Digression

Why do so many names for Internet functions suggest sexual, scatological, or rather degrading activities? Consider *Dogpile, Yahoo!, Excite, -crawler,* and *Carl UnCover.* Why do so many names for Internet matters suggest teenage slang or the language of hype (advertising, the shopping mall)? Think of *LitLink, Braintrack, Awesome List, Netsurfer, Bibliomania, BUBL Link,* and *INFOMINE.* Internet names, even for the most ponderous or sophisticated technical sites, frequently sound a bit silly, awestricken, naive, cool, lightly prurient, deliberately provocative in a mode that any parent of teenagers is apt to recognize. How very, very young the Internet is!

Subject Trees, Subject Guides, and Rating Sites

A *mere* subject tree has categories, subcategories, and sub-subcategories, and that is all, whereas a subject guide is a tree with annotations, ratings, or both. At the other extreme, a rating site has only ratings without necessarily relating them to a hierarchy of topics.

The two websites that are generally identified as the best subject trees for literary research are Alan Liu's *The Voice of the Shuttle* and Jack Lynch's *Online Literary Resources.* The latter is focused on subject matter that is identifiable as basic English Department stuff, whereas the former casts a wider net over all the Humanities subjects. Both give little or no clue to the content of their listings (links).

Some subject trees are much more general than these two; for example, *Yahoo!* and Netscape's own subject tree attempt to cover all the Internet topics, including art and literature, among categories such as Business, Entertainment, News, and Sports.

Other subject trees are much more specific, as mentioned earlier; some literary websites display subject trees as part of their approach to authors or periods. For example, *The Victorian Web* examines its authors under the categories Victorianism, Social Context, Economics, Religion, Philosophy, Literature, Visual Arts, Science, Technology, Politics, and Gender Matters.

Subject guides tend to be much more limited in coverage than subject trees simply because they provide more information, which is time consuming to amass. *Argus Clearinghouse,* for example, cannot begin to compare with *VOS* in terms of sheer numbers of links. *VOS* is clearly attempting to present at least one website for all the recognized authors in any given literary period, so when one uses *VOS* from the top down, it can be done with great assurance that the author for which one is searching will actually be there at the end of a twig. Not so with *Argus,* a subject guide with ratings meant to ensure the quality of the selected sites, sites that turn out to be very few in number. *Argus* has only fifteen sites under the literature category. It is nevertheless invaluable, sponsoring such sites as *Mr. William Shakespeare and the Internet,* the single most useful Shakespeare site—I dare say—on the World Wide Web.

Another very useful subject guide (without annotations but with ratings) is the *Malaspina Great Books Site* with links to a very long list of author pages that are all identified as Five Star Sites. Not all the sites are as very distinguished as that, but many deserve the recognition *Malaspina* gives them. Incidentally, *Malaspina Great Books,* unlike many of the other literary subject guides, is a commercial, not an educational, site cosponsored by *Amazon.com.* It seems to have no academic connections at all except to Malaspina University-College itself (located in British Columbia), but rather links to presses, libraries (not university libraries, but the Library of Congress and the National Library of Canada), the British Broadcasting Corporation (BBC), and online bookstores (Powell's and Blackwell's, in addition to Amazon); these institutions are the primary information and link sources for *Malaspina.* The chief problem with *Malaspina,* as with *Argus,* is that there is no assurance that a particular author will be there (for example, *Malaspina* lists sites for Aeschylus, Sophocles, and Aristophanes, while inexplicably omitting Euripides). But its standards are reasonably clear; it chooses as Five Star Sites those that "make effective and efficient use of authoritative WWW resources" and present information that "seems to be reliable." Perhaps the "seems to be" raises legitimate issues, but *Malaspina*'s choices are generally very useful literary sites, in any case.

In addition to subject guides with ratings, there are sites devoted altogether to rating other websites (more self-referentiality), literary and otherwise. Among these are *The Brittanica Internet Guide, Librarian's guide to the best information on the Net, Lycos Top 5%, Magellan,* and a regularly published Internet newsletter called *Netsurfer Digest.* All these ratings sites attempt to cover the entire range of subject matter on the net, so literature per se is only one of many concerns.

Internet critics have written quite unflattering reviews of the ratings sites themselves, suggesting that their standards are not clearly articulated, that their choices are inadequate, or that their practices or results are not as advertised. For example, some writers have objected to the *Lycos Top 5%* site because it claims on a continuing basis to uncover the top five percent of websites. How, ask the scoffers, can five percent of Internet sites be determined when it is widely stated that the exact number of sites on the Internet is impossible to discover? Certainly, it should be impossible to take five percent of an unknown number. Nevertheless, critics of ratings might bear the alternative in mind. Without the ratings systems (however inchoate or pretentious) and their websites, the selection of Internet sources becomes daunting to the *n*th degree, literally chaotic. Even the slightest effort to assess is a little helpful in a field where a lot of help is needed. If a person with a bit of liberal education makes a few informed judgments in rating Internet sites, that step should be welcomed, at least as a step in the right direction.

Single Search Engines

When scanning the long lists of search engines available on the net, lists that seem to grow longer every week, the user must wonder if all those mechanisms are really necessary. Are they really different from each other, or are they a prime example of computer redundancy? The answer to both questions is yes. Some of them are quite distinct, although others resemble their cohorts too closely to justify separate existence. (Search engines, of course, are not the only product in the marketplace about which such statements could be made). Search engines tend to be more commercial than subject trees in several senses: that is, they are usually sponsored by some company or companies, and commercials (advertisements) are almost always displayed with them.

Search engines come in two major varieties, which I call the single engine and the metaengine. A single-search engine, such as *AltaVista,* has its own database (enormous in this case; it is said to be the largest possessed by any of the search engines), its own parameters, its own rules of operation, and, not surprisingly, its own online tutorial. When given exactly the same information, single-search engines turn up different sites because the engines have different databases and because they search in very different ways. Sometimes, a particular search engine turns up nothing at all, whereas another single engine lists dozens of hits for exactly the same query.

AltaVista, like many other single-search engines, contains a subject tree or guide as well as a sophisticated search mechanism. As a subject tree, *AltaVista* is one of the very best; for example, in its Literature category (reached by clicking on "World" and then choosing the Reference and Education category, then Arts and Humanities), *AltaVista* offers an enormous further list of branches: Authors, Bestsellers and Reviews, Bookstores, Chat and Events, Countries and Cultures, Genres, Magazine and Journals, Online Texts, Poetry and Plays, Theory and Criticism, Writing and Publishing, and, finally, Best of the Web, an annotated list of superior literary sources. It is clear that *AltaVista*'s approach is popular rather than academic, so what it produces is an avid reader's guide, not a literary scholar's. Nevertheless, its subject tree is excellent and well worth exploring. Thus, *AltaVista,* once again like many other search engines, provides the opportunity to search from the top down.

Its primary function, however, is enabling particular searches; in addition to the simple search option, *AltaVista* provides several operations to refine specific searches, including use of various languages, a full range of Boolean expressions, and the choice of beginning and ending dates. The Help section gives instructions for using *AltaVista.* Stock Quotes, Yellow Pages, People Finder, and other specialty searches, none of them really of interest in literary terms, are also provided, along with links to *ABCNews.com, Amazon.com,* advertisers, sports, and so on.

None of these features is surprising in the wide world of search engines, although *AltaVista* may very well be the best of the lot. *Excite,* for example, is very limited compared with *AltaVista* and is wholly popular and personal as a subject guide, with built-in strategies for the user to personalize *Excite* as an opening home page. Books and Literature is a category subsumed under Entertainment in the *Excite* realm, as it is in *Lycos.* In any case, every popular single search engine has much the same features—besides a specific search engine, advertising, links, subject guides, some rating (more or less) system for sites—but the features in common do not indicate that all search engines are equal. *Thunderstone,* for a bad example, has an extensive, utterly eccentric subject guide that gives the user absolutely no clue concerning outcomes; the final branch of Literature (General) for *Thunderstone* ends in two twigs: (1) *The Ameen Rihami Home Page,* and (2) a site called simply *index.* I have not the slightest idea what these sites purport to be, but any searcher would, I believe, be surprised to run down such a blind alley.

Metasearch Engines

A metaseach engine combines the work of many single engines into one list of hits. For example, *Metacrawler,* one of the very best, at this moment uses *AltaVista, Excite, Infoseek, Lycos, Thunderstone, Webcrawler,* and *Yahoo!.* (I say "at this moment" because the list changes.) Because of the combinations, metasearch engines have to use the most general parameters available, and, in a sense, they perform lowest-common-denominator searches because they usually lack the fine tuning that can be applied within a single-search engine. Nevertheless, metasearchers are completely effective for most purposes; in most searches for literary sites, one metasearch engine is all that is ever required.

Metacrawler Searcher has no local database of its own but instead depends on the collections of its various web-based sources. It has very few advanced search options compared with *AltaVista,* for example, but it does offer the option of using quotes around words to lock them together as a search phrase, and it provides for Boolean expressions of plus and minus, at least. Nevertheless, limited as it may sound, *Metacrawler Searcher* is generally helpful for any sort of literary search from the bottom up, and it virtually ensures a useful sequence of hits on any subject. In its self-description, *Metacrawler* states that it "queries the other search engines, organizes the results into a uniform format, ranks them by relevance, and returns them to the user." I seldom use any other searching device, single or metasearch, because *Metacrawler* almost always delivers; when it does not, I typically turn to *AltaVista.*

The glaring deficiency of *Metacrawler* is in its subject guide; it has one, but it is very minimal. In fact, it seems that the subject tree is only there in structural imitation of the single engines. Searching from the top down in *Metacrawler* is really not an option.

CHAPTER 3

Kinds of Literary Websites

"PREVIOUSLY OWNED" ACADEMIC SITES

As already stated, many literary sites on the Internet consist of previously existing material fitted out with HTML tags and displayed on a convenient server. It is obvious that virtually all the literary works available on the Internet existed in print before they were placed on computer sites. These primary texts are, undoubtedly, the essential element of any literary presence on the net; their new, wider accessibility on the Internet is a boon to readers and scholars alike.

But other "previously owned" material is decidedly secondary, in both senses, even though some of it was widely accessible long before the advent of computers. Categories of such preexistent stuff include quite ordinary encyclopedia entries that usually still look exactly like what they are. Other pre-Internet works with an enormous presence on the Internet such as ordinary bibliographies (which, unfortunately, seem *inert* compared with webliographies with their linked entries) and a whole range of essays, theses, and dissertations reflect the growing use of the net by (even) grade school, high school, and college students, M.A. and Ph.D. candidates, and teachers. None of these latter productions necessarily enjoyed worldwide accessibility before a very few years ago, and why should they have? Is there any compelling reason why a freshman composition should be displayed for the entire world to see?

Nevertheless, all sorts of class assignments appear routinely on Internet sites. For many educators today, state-of-the-art instruction includes giving students their own home pages where homework may be displayed. Master's theses and Ph.D. writings are also commonplace, some (alas!) of an otherwise unpublishable quality.

Beginning at the top, the whole educational establishment creates Internet sites of preowned materials. College professors and high school teachers not only publish their essays and books, they also publish their lectures, syllabi, course guides, attendance policies, grading scales, selected bibliographies, and exams, among other things.

Students publish their assignments (using the word assignments to include even such lofty tasks as the dissertation), whatever they may be, plus lecture notes, negative vibes, and advice columns for those fated to suffer after them. More positively, they contribute the lion's share of academic fan sites, literary web pages generated from genuine enthusiasm. A few of these are among the best the Internet has to offer. The range of student publication is immense, partly because of the variety of their circumstances and ages, but also because students undertake both the most conservative and the most adventurous applications of Internet potentials. The impulse to *save* everything is clearly represented by the rush to publish every golden word the English major pens in college. The impulse to explore everything and—not surprisingly—to rebel against the establishment is also prominently displayed in literary sites where canon and pop culture, literary language and street slang jostle one another (more or less) comfortably.

Ironically, the use of the web for pedagogically sound educational purposes results in a cyberenvironment that is inimical to genuine Internet scholarship. The multiplication of inexpert sites, currently being promoted by computer-literate English departments all over the country (indeed, all over the world), requires a great deal of patience from an actual researcher who must weed through reams of students papers to find one page with some academic credentials. Although a sophomore's term paper on Emily Dickinson may be stimulating, it usually does not represent the height of scholarly insight and expertise, else what is the educational process intended to accomplish?

On the other hand, the only Internet sources for some authors, especially very contemporary, avant-garde, or—how do I put this?—very-distasteful-to-the-middle-class-sensibility authors, are student sites.

NONACADEMIC SITES

Booksellers, like educational establishments, have duly noted the importance of maintaining an Internet presence, and many combine advertising and information on sites that resemble immense collections of book jacket blurbs. But good blurbs should not be sold short: A visit to the Penguin Books sites (United Kingdom, United States, Canada, and Australia) turns out to be very educational for publication information, book descriptions, author biographies, book news, and so forth on three continents. Other institutions— nonacademic libraries, museums, public television stations, drama groups, awards organizations (the Nobel Prize, for example), foundations, literary societies, and fan clubs—sponsor a wealth of literary sites on the net.

A surprising number of literary societies devoted to single authors— Wilkie Collins, Thomas Paine, Jane Austen, William Dean Howells, Virginia Woolf, and Thomas Hardy, to name a few—offer unusual homage home pages with non–English department literary perspectives. Other societies operate from special convictions, deal only with authors who do the same, and cater to particular audiences: the Humanists, the Rationalists (yes, they have their own organizations with capital letters!), and especially feminists. Gay and lesbian sites usually announce their literary predilections in no uncertain terms. In practice, literary society sites have an indiscernible boundary with fan club sites, which segue into individual fan sites.

Fan sites—defined as the work of authors who are not motivated by formal educational demands—are designed by amateurs, but they are not always amateurish. Sometimes they are personal pages produced by (1) people trained in the actual discipline but not working within an institutional framework, (2) amateurs (lovers) of great expertise and singular dedication, or (3) computer specialists with other interests. Fan pages are also at times the work of idiots.

Fan sites are ubiquitous on the Internet (and not just in literature, of course). Any author or period may incur fan sites, but certain writers are more apt to attract them than others. Shakespeare has thousands, Jane Austen and Emily Dickinson have a great many, Edgar Allan Poe has at least his share. How *do* authors incur their web treatments? A study could be made: Caryl Churchill sites constructed from female undergraduate term papers; Chinua Achebe represented by class assignments in World Literature; rabid fan sites in favor of Emily Dickinson for all seasons; genteel, gentle Janeite sites; William Shakespeare with a vast flood of pages instantly replicating and extending the glut of work already done concerning him. Beyond our expectations, other literary figures have unique fan pages of their very own: Dylan Thomas is a great favorite of the Australians, with two fan sites located there, whereas Margaret Atwood has a well-maintained Canadian fan site.

An unusual kind of special interest literary site is the tourist site, usually equipped with images of literary locales, sometimes accompanied by local interest stories, promotional material, and sales pitches. Writers attached to particular places are liable to inspire tourist home pages in both the United States and Great Britain: Sherwood Anderson, for example, is the subject of sites originating from northern Ohio (where he grew up) and Smyth County, Virginia (where he worked briefly); William Faulkner is enshrined in tourist sites from Mississippi; and Flannery O'Connor is exhibited from Georgia. Lyme Regis, the Lake Country, the Yorkshire moors, and especially (you guessed it!) Stratford and the Globe Theatre link writers and places. A good site to sample is *Dorset's Literary Connections,* with links to both literary and geographical connections. Literary pilgrimage sites are sometimes very beautiful, but—as in pre-Internet days—their spiels smack of the Chamber of Commerce, adding to the underlying sense that authors, periods, books, and whatever are always being advertised, touted, marketed, and sold on the net.

A large-scale, general site devoted to literary places is *Literary Locales,* with dozens of images of places with literary connections, from Tony Hillerman's Country to Chaucer's Canterbury. Although much of the material on such a site existed before the Internet was in use, it seems to be displayed more effectively and conveniently on the net than anywhere else. Still other productions that benefit from computer display are chronologies of literature, literary calendars, and timelines, all of which use clickable links and colorful layouts to great advantage.

AUTHOR SITES

The most numerous kind of literary source on the Internet is the simple, single-author biographical site. By far the most prevalent kind of author site consists of (usually) a picture of the author, a brief (sometimes ludicrously brief) biographical sketch with no indication of its source, and a list of links. (Actually, the typical author site, except for its links, is very much like an author's bio and picture on a book flap.)

The lowest common denominator of authors and links pages (and there is at least one of these for virtually every author anyone has ever heard of before last week) is the encyclopedia entry from online works such as *Encarta* and *Encyclopedia.com.* These are the author pages with the smallest biographies and the most limited links, most of them within the encyclopedia site itself.

A fully developed author page on the net, however, may provide invaluable context. *Luminarium,* for example, devotes a major site to every well-known English author from the Middle Ages through the seventeenth century, with copious links, reliable notes, beautiful images, and period music.

Some author-devoted pages go well beyond biography, as in the *F. Scott Fitzgerald Centenary Page* and *The Henry James Scholar's Guide to Web Sites,* which attempt to cover *all* the areas of possible Internet research for a given writer.

In searching the Internet for individual authors, the researcher is frequently impeded by the vast number of author sites and by their redundancy. Many author pages are not quite but almost exactly alike, so it may appear from a list of hits that one has uncovered twenty different sites on Cervantes, when on closer examination the number of really distinct sites turns out to be two.

Some author sites omit both picture and biography and provide only the links, in tacit acknowledgment that the links are usually the most significant part of the author-bio-links page schema. Some of those links are exclusively to e-texts of the author's works. In any case, for the majority of writers virtually all Internet sources are biographical. One is much more apt to see an author page than a site that is work- or period-oriented or than a site with a genre or other contextual orientation. Thus, the web by default promotes an auteur approach in literature, an issue that will receive more attention in Chapter 9. The Internet literary world is divided into famous authors who may (or must) be approached through biographical criticism, much as in the nineteenth century.

DEPARTMENTS AND LIBRARIES

University and college home pages (.edu sites) sponsor some literary resources that are not the province of teachers, courses, and students. Departmental pages, for example, frequently present general Internet bibliographies for their clientele and anyone else who visits the site; some of the best webliographies (a webliography is a bibliography that has every item linked to the actual source named; it is the most convenient form of bibliography invented thus far) occur as parts of English, classics, or (more rarely) history department home pages.

The other academic resource that transcends pre-Internet materials is library related. Reference librarians have become a real power on the academic Internet, with some of the best known and most useful sites maintained by individual librarians (such as *Best Information on the Net—English or English and American Literature: Internet Resources*). Librarians set the pace and the standards for Internet research in general, and their research standards are being applied within literary studies as never before. Some librarian work— for instance, the many sources concerning search engines—is rather too technical and detailed to be generally useful. It is safe to expect, however, that library sites will display solid work, up-to-date maintenance, well-chosen links, and a high level of general research expertise. Since all this helpful work by librarians has been done in response to the Internet, it represents one of the largest, most important segments of what is genuinely new because of the net.

BOOKSTORES, PUBLISHERS, AND PERIODICALS

Bookstores, academic publishing companies, and periodicals have also begun producing new materials and techniques through the Internet. *Amazon.com,* for example, has many features that an "actual" bookstore could scarcely emulate: its immense searchable list of books in stock, used, rare, and so forth and, especially, its reader review section. Rarely has the ordinary reader been offered such a forum, offered as much *say* as can be exercised at *Amazon.com.* Has such a collection of ordinary reader (nonacademic, not necessarily college age) responses ever existed before? I think not. For example, when I was asked to write a review of *Cold Mountain,* I checked *Amazon.com*'s reader reviews to see if I could get some inkling of why the novel had achieved and kept its bestseller status. Hundreds of reviews—many of them eloquent, knowledgable, and involved—were online, and they constituted what no academic would have predicted. They were an extremely useful documentation of what actual readers actually think and feel, what they notice, and how they interpret texts.

In addition, *Amazon.com* works very well as an online substitute for *Books in Print,* itself online only as a subscription service; practically speaking, *Amazon.com* provides more reliable reporting on whether a given book is actually available. The electronic bookstore also sponsors some fine work on other sites, such as *Malaspina Great Books* and *Luminarium.*

Academic publishers (and other publishers too) supply online book news and descriptions, summaries, and advertisements of their offerings, just as one might expect, but they have moved beyond the content and style of their "actual" promotional material into more elaborate and thorough treatments on site after site of authors, periods, and pedagogical possibilities. Textbook publishers have developed some very helpful sites (Bedford Books, for example) keyed to their own anthologies.

Many publishers of academic periodicals, even those not presenting current issues online and thus competing with themselves, present archives of older issues on the Internet. Some periodicals actually place versions of their regular publications online, whereas still others (for example) exist *only* online.

All three of these Internet producers have boundaries with limited access, subscription sites, and CD-ROMs. For example, *Amazon.com,* perhaps inadvertently, gives away what *Books in Print* demands payment for. Some journals are free online, whereas others require subscription fees, and only promotional material—however elaborate—from publishers is given away on the net. These juxtapositions are rather like another electronic relationship: that between ordinary free TV and various (multiplying) subscription services. As more and more sophisticated, "unique," and marketable literary sites are developed, it is likely that more and more of them will require a password or membership, a fee (sometimes so hefty only an institution can afford it), or extra software or equipment.

As there are preexistent Internet materials and materials produced only in response to the net, so are there also institutions both pre- and postInternet. *Amazon.com* itself is, of course, a case in point. There are many other instances of societies and organizations that exist only on and because of the Internet.

IMAGES AND MUSIC

The Internet has the interesting capacity to link text with images and sound, so sites that emphasize such connections are becoming one of the most attractive, new resources of the web. *Luminarium* sites, for example, offer both carefully selected images and musical interludes on both the general links pages and on individual author sites. On Ben Jonson's page, the user hears a ballad called "The Three Ravens." A beautiful electronic edition of Shakespeare's *Venus and Adonis* is adorned with images of paintings, sculptures, and illustrations inspired by the story.

Images and designs occur everywhere on the Internet, of course, and they are mostly incidental (the user can even decide to switch them off to facilitate more rapid downloading of text), but for some pages—Balzac portraits on an author page, book covers of editions of Dante published during the Renaissance, William Blake's illustrations for *Songs of Innocence and Experience* —they really are an integral part of the offering or even the main thing. Photographic and cinematic images are also exploited, for example, in such sites as *Arts and History—Juan Rulfo* and *Tennessee Williams on the Web Photo Gallery.*

The Internet excels at sources based on visual images of actual texts, such as the *Electronic Beowulf, Renaissance Dante in Print (1472–1629),* and *Classic Text: Traditions and Interpretations,* which features important editions of the Bible and works by Homer, Aristophanes, Virgil, Ovid, Saint Augustine, Dante, Chaucer, Spenser, Shakespeare, Milton, James Fenimore Cooper, Nathaniel Hawthorne, Harriet Beecher Stowe, and James Joyce. Some sites devoted to Shakespeare editions such as the first Folio of *Hamlet* and the second Quarto of *King Lear*, both presented by the University of Pennsylvania Library's *Center for Electronic Text and Image (CETI),* represent state-of-the-art computer imaging.

LINKS PAGES

The three most distinctive sorts of literary sites are probably links pages, webrings, and projects, all of which are rendered *possible* by the special capacities of the Internet itself. It is important to realize the distinction between materials that are merely rendered more accessible by the Internet (even when their accessibility is scarcely desirable, such as term papers) and those that are actually made possible only by the Internet. In my view, the latter represent the only distinctive contributions that the net has made or is likely to make in the field of literature. Accessibility, after all, only depends on quantity.

Links pages are precisely what the name indicates. They are sites that have no interest at all in themselves, because they only present links to other sites. Some links pages are random assortments; most today are supremely hierarchical in structure with categories, subcategories, and subsubcategories, frequently immense exercises in analyzing and classifying, and presorted electronic bibliographies.

Some come complete with brief descriptions of the sites linked, some few present annotations, and even fewer attempt some form of rating. It is not unusual, however, for a links page to be a list of names of sites *only.* Even in that form, a links page may be one of the most valuable Internet resources. An incalculable number of links pages is already on Internet display, and the number grows daily.

WEBRINGS

Webrings are an Internet invention, useful for both users and contributors. A webring is a circle of sites that, once entered, allows the user to access all the pages within a set. Frequently, a site in a webring has a clickable link called "next site in the webring"; if the user consistently clicks that link on site after site, she will eventually circle though the entire ring and return to the starting point. Since webrings are usually devoted to particular subjects, the user can choose a webring devoted to a topic of general interest and explore it electronically and, in some cases, very thoroughly. Period webrings are a very notable concept in literary sites in collections such as the *Baroque Ring* and the *18th Century Ring*.

Webrings require membership applications from those who would like to join them as contributors. To some extent, peer review may be applied as webrings widen their circle, but that is not necessarily the case. The user must check the rules for each individual webring to see what standards, if any, are applied.

PROJECTS

Projects, some of which are the glory of the literary Internet, are frequently distinctive contributions in joint scholarship, imaginative vision, and artistic design. Usually sponsored by academic institutions or major cultural organizations, they tend to be long-term activities, so that they are often works in progress even when they have exceeded some completed sites in both content and design. Many scholars may be associated with a literary Internet project, sometimes as actual contributors, designers, editorial board members, or fund-raisers. Such sites as the *Perseus Project, Romantic Chronology, Romantic Circles,* the *Camelot Project* (with texts, images, bibliographies, and basic information, sponsored by the University of Rochester), the *Sor Juana Project,* the *Dickens Project,* the *Walt Whitman Hypertext Archive,* and the *Dickinson Electronic Archive* offer, in many cases, multimedia sites of great academic importance.

Because they are highly designed and highly visible as aspects of academic and institutional research, many of the well-known projects are unique, providing information and connections that are not available in the world at large, no more accessible in the ordinary library than any special archival material would be, and no more redundant than careful scholarship in any media.

When academics extol the virtues of the Internet in their own fields, they frequently seem to have projects in mind, not the run-of-the-mill, dime-a-dozen author pages, not the collections of freshmen themes, not even the webliographies. In many cases, projects represent the highest form of literary scholarship applied within the new electronic media.

THE BREAKING OF LITERARY HIERARCHIES

Although the projects may be the Internet's most notable achievement in literary scholarship, its primary consequence in the literary field is the breaking up of age-old hierarchies, but not, I hasten to add, in the sense of departing from any canonical traditions. The Internet maintains the canon in some respects much more forcefully than the other world does. Classical, canonical literature seems intact, and every work that is considered part of the traditional selection has a presence on the Internet; our bibliography of websites, which follows, proves that point.

But the literary canon on the Internet is maintained within a very unusual framework (that is, a very unusual framework as far as academics are concerned). Literature on the Internet is associated with every kind of context and every level of readership. The confines of academe and high cultural institutions have been breached; the old assumptions about where the study of literature belongs are crumbling.

Advertising, pornography (at least, omnipresent erotic suggestions), entertainment, business, television, the news, and the weather all intrude or provide welcome relief in almost any Internet exploration, literary or not. All literary sites are not .edu (educational); some are .org (organizational), some are .gov (governmental), and some are even .com (commercial). The mix is overt and complete; to some academics it may seem to be an instance of sacred cows lodged in the Augean stables.

Literature, *great* literature, is appearing in the context of the very latest, new electronic marvels and the very oldest aspects of the "real," as opposed to the academic, world. Literature is being both leveled and exalted, I would say.

In addition, the Internet has put literature into a context of every level of readership. The breaking of the hierarchical includes the question of who is now discussing, critiquing, or responding to and analyzing literature in "print," all over the net. Traditional *critics* are scarce on the Internet, but criticism of another sort is finding its popular voice in discussion groups, on listservs, on fan pages, and in such forums as *Amazon.com*'s reader comment sites.

The leveling performed by the Internet is related to the realization that ordinary people read great books and comment on them, even love them. Their critical writing is going on, as it almost always has, in a cultural matrix far from the academic realm. The breaking of hierarchies has not been (so far) a rearrangement of works, but of contexts and readers. It may be that this new development will produce results of a surprising sort. There is, after all, no particular evidence that academics enjoy reading books more than non-degree-seeking people do. Might the Internet actually increase our potential for *enjoying* literature? Could pleasure once again become a viable reason for reading? Surely, in all seriousness, reading habits and standards will be re-shaped as the influence of the Internet on literature increases. Writing and composition itself may be altered, too. Maybe even now a great writer is being prepared, a writer whose influences are derived from the Internet, and whose publications will appear on the Internet, whose critical reputation and audience will develop there as well. Academics may not be privileged to be the first to recognize this new Shakespeare, as, indeed, they were not in the late sixteenth century.

CHAPTER 4

Literary Guide to the Internet: A Bibliography

The following annotated bibliography of Internet sources is based on two previous compilations: one is simply a required reading list for English majors at Berea College and the other a literary webliography <http://www.berea.edu/ENG/ENG.home.html#Webliography> that appears as part of the English departmental home page for the same institution. Like its sources, this bibliography aims at offering a broad range of literary resources on the net. The departmental reading list was used as a starting point to ensure breadth of coverage: every period, most well-known authors, all genres, and so on. The goal was to locate at least one reasonably useful Internet source for every major writer included on the reading list, and that task was completed without a single exception. Likewise, a conscious effort was made to present at least one example of every *kind* of literary resource available on the Internet. Thus, this bibliography represents the full range of pre-Internet literary subjects while at the same time exploring the full range of sources specific to the Internet.

For every entry the most interesting site has been chosen, and in most instance choices were available. For some authors—those from the Spanish Renaissance, for example—however, only one source could be found, usually from an Internet encyclopedia, the lowest common denominator of Internet sites. These entries are of no particular importance individually, but they are included because it is essential for users to see that absolutely every literary topic is already represented by some site on the Internet.

It is impossible to assess literary websites by some absolute standard, but the various uses to which these resources might be put have been imagined, bearing in mind the diverse purposes of teachers and college students at many different levels of expertise. Some sources have been selected because they clearly represent a very high degree of scholarship with impeccable academic credentials, others because they represent established approaches or views, others because they demonstrate how actual readers react to literature, still others because they display beautiful graphics or remarkable searchability and convenience or an immense selection of links or because they show how eccentric the offspring of traditonal literature and contemporary technology can be.

Items of exceptional merit or interest (however those qualities are defined) are marked with two asterisks, and every item is annotated based on the experience of an actual visit or visits to the site. Thus, it may be assumed that every item on the bibliography is actually in existence and is currently accessible. Websites, however, are notorious for coming and going, so no absolute guarantee can be offered. Some items will have disappeared by the time this book is printed, and some will have entered the realm of pay-per-view subscription sites. Other sites will remain at the cited URLs, but they will be revised out of recognition. The annotator of Internet sites has the Heraclitean (and Herculean) task of describing a river that changes perpetually.

Nevertheless, many of the sources listed have achieved the status of the expected source. Users know them and count on them; changing them would call forth a public outcry of protests. *The Voice of the Shuttle*, for example, changes all the time while maintaining the same standards and the same basic patterns of arrangement and satisfying the same research goals. Many other sites display a high degree of permanence structurally, even though they may post quotidian changes.

The primary value of this bibliography is not its addresses, annotations or ratings—although all these should prove useful—but that virtually every literary resource on the entire Internet is within one click from some item included. It is not just a gateway to the literary Internet; it is a full-scale exploration from which every area of the superstructure, even obscure corners, is in sight.

1. LITERARY INTERNET RESOURCES: WEBLIOGRAPHIES, BIBLIOGRAPHIES, AND GUIDES

English: General Sites for Literature

ABELL: Home Page
http://www.lib.cam.ac.uk/MHRA/ABELL/
> Information about the Annual Bibliography of English Language and Literature (ABELL) on the Modern Humanities Research Association site, Cambridge University.

Argus Clearinghouse Literature Links
http://www.clearinghouse.net/cgi-bin/chadmin/viewcat/Arts___Humanities/
literature?kywd++
> Links to literary sites approved by *Argus*, including American literature, Book collecting, children's literature, fiction, Shakespeare, and world literature.

Bedford Books: Literature Links, Alphabetical List of Authors
http://www.bedfordbooks.com/litlinks/alpha.html
> Very useful list of annotated links for the (quite substantial) group of authors published by Bedford Books.

Best Information on the Net—English
http://www.saUniversityedu/CWIS/Internet/Wild/Majors/English/litindex.htm
> Very useful page of annotated literary links chosen by the librarians of O'Keefe Library, St. Ambrose University; constantly updated.

**Classic Text, The: Traditions and Interpretations
http://www.uwm.edu/Dept/Library/special/exhibits/clastext/clshome.htm
> Site based on an exhibit at the Golda Meir Library, University of Wisconsin–Milwaukee; presentation and analysis of text editions, mostly of classical works; images and commentary.

Dorset's Literary Connections
http://home.sprynet.com/sprynet/btomp/literary.htm
> Part of the Dorset Page; links to authors who lived, wrote, or vacationed in Dorsetshire; straightforward tourist site.

EducETH—The English Page
http://educeth.ethz.ch/english/
> General all-purpose site compiling information for students and teachers of English throughout the world; emphasis on assignments, discussions, reading lists, sharing resources.

Electronic Archives for Teaching the American Literatures, The
http://www.georgetown.edu/tamlit/tamlit-home.html
> Links provided by Georgetown University and Heath Publishing Company; features essays, syllabi, bibliographies, and other resources for teaching the multiple literatures of the United States.

English and American Literature: Internet Resources
http://www2.lib.udel.edu/subj/engl/internet.htm
> Many categories of annotated links from the University of Delaware Library.

English and Humanities Related Links
http://www.english.udel.edu/humanities/
> Links page of the English Department of the University of Delaware; especially good for organizations, such as MLA and SAMLA.

English Literature and Composition Resources on the Internet: Selected Sites
http://www.iat.unc.edu/guides/irg-30.html
> Links site maintained by Carolyn Kotlas at Institute for Academic Technology with sections devoted to literature, composition and rhetoric,

writing centers, and more; reviewed in *Choice: Current Reviews for Academic Libraries*.

English Server Drama Collection
http://eserver.org/drama/
> Mostly a collection of plays and screenplays, although some critical works are included; texts range from ancient Greek to modern; links to other sources and a search engine; reviewed in *Choice*.

Guide to Theater Resources on the Internet
http://www-old.ircam.fr/divers/theatre-e.html
> Enormous source with an index page spreading over eighteen pages; numerous links to Shakespeare, theater discussion groups, performance studies, theater theory, archives, Usenet newsgroups, and many more.

Heath Anthology: Syllabus Builder, Version 2.0: Instructor's Guide for The Heath Anthology of American Literature
http://www.georgetown.edu/bassr/heath/syllabuild/iguide/
> Enormous list of links to authors and periods of the Heath Anthology; study guides; helpful in planning courses and choosing assignments.

History of the English Language Home Page, The
http://ebbs.english.vt.edu/hel/hel.html
> Many links divided into categories of linguistic development (Prehistory, Old English, Middle English, American and present-day Englishes); course syllabi included.

****Internet Sites for Choice Magazine*
http://www.jsUniversityedu/depart/english/choice.htm
> List providing links to sites discussed in an essay by Joanne Gates, "Literature in Electronic Format: the Traditional English and American Canon" in *Choice* (April 1997); very thorough, useful subject tree.

Internet Guide to English Resources
http://www.wmin.ac.uk/IRS/EC/ECLIB/english.html
> Annotated links from the University of Westminster.

Internet Links to Major English Subject Tree Collections
http://www.ulib.csuohio.edu/eng-m.html
> Links (mostly unannotated, but in useful categories) from the Cleveland State University Library.

IPL Online Literary Criticism Collection Main Page
http://www.ipl.org/ref/litcrit/
> The Internet Public Library's selection of 1,401 critical and biographical websites about authors and their works; browsable by author, title, or literary period.

Literary Calendar: An Almanac of Literary Information
http://litcal.yasuda-Universityac.jp/LitCalendar.shtml
> Calendar of clickable dates linked to literary events; short entries for each day of the current month; links to authors; presented by Yasuda Women's University.

Literary Lists
http://www-stat.wharton.upenn.edu/~siler/litlists.html
> Links to home pages for literary prizes for fiction: Booker Prize, Nobel Prize, American Fiction Awards, and so on.

Literary Locales
http://www.sjsUniversityedu/depts/english/places.htm
> Picture links to places that figure in the lives and writings of famous authors; worldwide coverage; maintained by the Department of English at San Jose State University.

Literary Terms and Rhetorical Devices
http://www.uky.edu/ArtsSciences/Classics/Harris/rhetform.html
> "A Glossary of Literary Terms" and "A Handbook of Rhetorical Devices" by Robert Harris, professor of English at South California College; search capability and indexes.

Literature, Arts, and Medicine Database
http://endeavor.med.nyUniversityedu/lit-med/lit-med-db/topview.html
> Annotated bibliography of prose, poetry, film, video, and art; developed as an accessible, comprehensive resource in medical humanities; maintained by an editorial board at New York University's School of Medicine.

Literature Online Home Page
http://lion.chadwyck.com/
> Adjunct to Chadwyck-Healey's subscription site.

****Literature Webliography*
http://www.lib.lsUniversityedu/hum/lit.html
> Very thorough, extensive subject guide produced by Louisiana State University with annotated links to general guides, bibliographies, library catalogs, dictionaries, discussions, organizations, periodicals, style guides, and electronic texts as well as individual authors.

LitLinks
http://www.ualberta.ca/~amactavi/litlinks.htm
> Links page from the University of Alberta with some unusual categories: theory, literary, hypertext, cultural, humanities and computing, and gender issues.

****Luminarium*

http://www.luminarium.org/lumina.htm

> Beautiful, reliable, award-winning site devoted to English literature (medieval through seventeenth century); maintained by Anniina Jokinen and sponsored by the Luminarium Bookstore; many external links, but not identified as such, that connect to sites of varying quality; reviewed in *Choice*.

****Malaspina Great Books Home Page—Five Star Sites*

http://www.mala.bc.ca/~mcneil/fivestar.htm

> Large list of links to rated sites concerning writers, musicians, artists, philosophers, and others; a few sites do not live up to expectations, but many deserve their five stars; very helpful in literature area; maintained by Russell McNeil, Ph.D., at Malaspina University-College.

Online Archive of California, The

http://sunsite2.berkeley.edu/oac/

> Collaborative project of the University of California, Berkeley, and Sun Microsystems; offers links to excellent sites for the major university and research libraries in California.

****On-Line Literary Resources*

http://dept.english.upenn.edu/~jlynch/lit/

> Jack Lynch's subject tree/search engine page with links leading to dozens more; reviewed by *Choice*; generally considered one of the two most useful literary resource sites (the other is *Voice of the Shuttle*).

Perspectives in American Literature

http://www.csustan.edu/english/reuben/home.htm#book

> Access to "Perspectives on American Literature: A Research and Reference Guide" by Paul P. Reuben, professor of English at California State University; linked topic by topic; with syllabi and other resources.

San Antonio College LitWeb Index, The

http://www.accd.edu/sac/english/bailey/litindex.htm

> Departmental links page maintained by Professor Roger Blackwell Bailey.

****SHARP Web*

http://www.indiana.edu/~sharp/

> Home page for the Society for the History of Authorship, Reading and Publishing; enormous list of links to sites dealing with the history of books, publishing, and so forth; unique site with a new range of literary applications.

Voices & Visions Spotlight

http://www.learner.org/collections/multimedia/literature/vvseries/vvspot/index.html

Associated with a video series, part of the Annenberg/CPB project; links to sites for thirteen modern American poets, including Eliot, Hughes, Dickinson, Crane, Moore, Frost, Bishop, and Lowell.

English Resources: Composition

Computer Writing and Research Labs
http://www.cwrl.utexas.edu/
Site maintained by the Division of Rhetoric and Composition at the University of Texas at Austin; links to online courses, resources, computer writing and research labs e-journal; multi-user environments, discussion forums, and a search engine.

Inkspot: Writing Resources, Newsletter for Writers
http://www.inkspot.com/
Reviewed in *Choice*.

National Writing Centers Association, The
http://departments.colgate.edu/diw/NWCA.html
Site maintained by Bruce Pegg, director of Colgate University's Writing Center; links to writing center resources, tutor stories, writing centers online, e-mail discussion groups, resources for writers, electronic and print journals, and more; reviewed in *Choice*.

On-line English Grammar
http://www.edunet.com/english/grammar/index.cfm
Site authored byAnthony Hughes in conjunction with St. John's Wood School of English in London; grammar text with links to table of contents, subject index, and other resources; reviewed in *Choice*.

Online Writing Lab, Purdue University.
http://owl.english.purdue.edu/
Web page adjunct of Purdue University's actual lab, with links to other writing labs, resources for writers, resources for teachers, and Internet seach tools; reviewed in *Choice*.

Reference Sources: British and UniversityS. Literature
http://www.haverford.edu/library/reference/rkieft/SENENG1.html
Materials geared toward the research paper.

UVic Writer's Guide, The
http://elza.lpi.ac.ru/WritersGuide/welcome.html
Linked glossary of literary and rhetorical terms; examples of usage from literary works; originally prepared for students by the English Department at the University of Victoria.

WritersNet: Internet Resource for Writers, Editors, Publishers and Agents
http://www.writers.net/

Home page designed for published writers and aspiring authors; convenient site map with an overview of resources, including a link to literary
agents.

Online Literary Journals, Hypertext Fiction, and Poetry

Alsop Review, The
http://www.hooked.net/~jalsop/index.html
    Online contemporary poetry review.

Atlantic Unbound/The Atlantic Monthly
http://www.theatlantic.com/index-js.htm
    Part of the *Literary Arts Webring.*

Books in Chains
http://www.uc.edu/~rettbesr/links.html
    Enormous list of annotated literary links by an enthusiast named Scott
    Rettberg at the University of Cincinnati.

Boston Book Review Home Page
http://www.bookwire.com/bbr/bbr-home.html
    Online journal of book reviews and essays, covering many categories of
    books; sponsored by *BookWire.*

Chronicle of Higher Education, The
http://thisweek.chronicle.com/"
    E-publication, updated constantly; the user is informed of news and re-
    cent features; information includes news on books, publications, educa-
    tion, and information technology.

Diacritics Home Page
http://jhupress.jhUniversityedu/journals/diacritics/
    Part of Project Muse, offering online texts of volumes of *Diacritics,* a
    journal with critical and scholarly essays.

Electronic Journals
http://www.edoc.com/ejournal
    Links page to various categories of electronic journals, including acade-
    mic and reviewed, college or university, e-mail newsletters, and maga-
    zines and newspapers.

Electronic Journals and Other Electronic Publications
http://www.lib.lsUniversityedu/local.html
    Links page with connections to electronic text archives, general list of
    journals and so forth, and Louisiana State University's electronic journal
    publications.

Electronic Poetry Center Home Page
http://wings.buffalo.edu/epc/
   Site at the State University of New York at Buffalo with an alphabetical
   list of poets, critics, and writers in hypertext; lists of poetry magazines,
   both electronic and print, poetry presses, and other e-poetry sites.

English Server, The
http://english-server.hss.cmUniversityedu/
   Based in the English Department at Carnegie Mellon University; publishes writings and artwork (over 20,000 works) for online readers; reviewed in *Choice*.

Enterzone
http://ezone.org/ez/enterzone.html
   Arts and literary e-zine with many innovative features and a laid-back
   style; each issue is (perhaps rightly) called an episode; archive of back
   numbers.

Harvard Advocate Online, The
http://www.hcs.harvard.edu/~advocate/
   Online version of the oldest continuously publishing college literary
   magazine in the United States.

Henry James Review Home Page, The
http://muse.jhUniversityedu/journals/henry_james_review/
   Many back issues available online for subscribers to Project Muse.

**Hyperizons: Hypertext Fiction*
http://www.duke.edu/~mshumate/hyperfic.html
   Extensive hyperlinked list to authors' home pages, hypertext fiction, theorists, publishers, and resources for all things related to hypertext fiction.

Iowa Review, The
http://www.uiowa.edu/~english/iowareview/
   Home page that includes contents and excerpts from previous editions of
   the *Iowa Review*.

John Labovitz's E-zine-list
http://www.meer.net/~johnl/e-zine-list/index.html
   Comprehensive list of e-zines around the world, accessible via the web,
   file transfer protocol (FTP), e-mail, and other services; maintained since
   1993 and updated constantly; 2,537 entries at last count.

Kairos Shell
http://english.ttUniversityedu/kairos/1.1/index.html
   Online journal for teachers of writing in webbed environments.

Keats–Shelley Journal Home Page
http://www.luc.edu/publications/keats-shelley/ksjweb.htm
> Internet adjunct to the print journal (not the publication itself), with contents of previous issues; links to web resources and Keats–Shelley bibliography.

Literary Arts WebRing, The—Index of Members
http://www.lit-arts.com/WebRing/RingIndex.html
> Community of websites "representing the very best the web has to offer in the art, craft, and business of fiction, poetry, essays, and creative nonfiction"; e-journals include *Atlantic Unbound, The Blue Moon Review, Conjunctions,* and *Grand Street.*

Milton Quarterly, The
http://voyager.cns.ohioUniversityedu/~somalley/milton.html
> Adjunct to the print journal with links to a very interesting set of online resources.

Mississippi Review
http://www.sonances.qc.ca/journals/mississippi.htm
> Part of the *Literary Arts WebRing.*

Missouri Review, The: Fiction, Poetry, Essays, Features, and Interviews
http://www.missouri.edu/~moreview/
> Part of the *Literary Arts WebRing.*

OBR/Oyster Boy Review
http://helios.oit.unc.edu/ob/index.html
> Print and online journal of fiction and poetry; among the links are the Jargon Society, dedicated to "publishing the overlooked and the underrated."

Ploughshares
http://www.emerson.edu/ploughshares/
> Part of the *Literary Arts WebRing.*

Poetry Webring
http://www.webring.org/cgi-bin/webring?ring=poetry;list
> A WebRing of 3,087 connected sites, each devoted to poetry composed by the owners of those home pages; an immense source for viewing contemporary poetic sensibility; by far the most popular webring among those listed by *RingWorld: Arts and Humanities.*

Quarterly Black Review of Books, The
http://www.bookwire.com/qbr/qbr.html
> *BookWire* online review site focused on books by African-American authors and about African-American people; many links, including a notable one to a guide to Black classics.

RingWorld: Arts and Humanities/Literature
http://www.webring.org/ringworld/arts/hum.html
> Huge linked list of webrings; most usual subjects are genre literatures (science fiction, fantasy, romance, erotica, children's fiction) and writing groups, especially circles of practicing Internet poets.

Shakespeare Quarterly, The
http://www.folger.edu/academic/sq/menUniversityhtm
> Not an online version, but displays links to tables of contents of issues from 1995, plus a link to information about the World Shakespeare Bibliography.

Spark, an Online Literary Review
http://wwwenglish.ucdavis.edu/spark/default.html
> Fiction and poetry by the students, alumni, and faculty of the Graduate Creative Writing Program at the University of California at Davis.

War, Literature, and the Arts
http://www.usafa.af.mil/dfeng/wla/"
> International journal of the humanities, published by the English Department of the United States Air Force Academy.

Web Del Sol
http://webdelsol.com/
> Fiction, poetry, and essay selections from small presses and literary journals; information for writers; attractive and knowledgable site about contemporary literary arts.

ZIPZAP E-ZINE
http://www.dnai.com/~zipzap/zissue3/contents.html
> Back issues (to 1996) of what was obviously intended as a very contemporary, even avant-garde, review of fiction and poetry; rather self-consciously peculiar.

Encyclopedias

Britannica Online
http://www.eb.com/
> By subscription only.

Encarta® Online Home
http://encarta.msn.com/encartahome.asp
> Free version of *Encarta's Encyclopedia;* concise edition still includes 16,000 articles.

Encyclopedia.com from Electric Library
http://www.encyclopedia.com/

More than 17,000 articles from the *Concise Columbia Electronic Encyclopedia.*

New Advent: The Catholic Encyclopedia
http://www.knight.org/advent/cathen/
> Transcriptions of entries from the *Catholic Encyclopedia* presented by enthusiast Kevin Knight and volunteers; links to separate volumes.

2. LITERARY PERIODS, GROUPS, AND GENRES

Classical

Ancient World Web: Main Index, The
http://www.julen.net/aw/
> Master index to all entries in the source, geography index, subject index, additional search engines and indices, and frequently asked questions; extremely effective, easy-to-use research tool; links to a staggering number of sources concerning ancient cultures.

Diotima: Women and Gender in the Ancient World
http://www.uky.edu/ArtsSciences/Classics/gender.html
> Course-related site from the University of Kentucky with links to course materials, bibliographies, and visual images; very recently updated; reviewed in *Choice.*

Epic Web Pages
http://www.sjc.ox.ac.uk/users/gorney/
> Site presenting various perspectives on Greek and Latin epics; maintained by Laura Gorney, apparently a classics student at Oxford.

Internet Classics Archive: 441 Searchable Works of Classical Literature
http://classics.mit.edu/
> A list of 441 searchable works by fifty-nine classical authors; sponsored by the Massachusetts Institute of Technology Program in Writing and Humanistic Studies; reviewed by *Choice.*

Library of Congress Resources for Greek and Latin Classics
http://lcweb.loc.gov/global/classics/classics.html
> Links to the classics collections of the Library of Congress and to a Vatican exhibit; reviewed in *Choice.*

**Perseus Project Home Page
http://www.perseus.tufts.edu/
> Tufts University's elaborate, immensely attractive, thorough site dedicated to the study of ancient Greek civilization; links to art and archaelogy as well as texts, secondary sources, teaching suggestions; reviewed in *Choice.*

Related Readings: Classics and Ancient World
http://jefferson.village.virginia.edu/readings/classics.html
    A links-only page sponsored by the University of Virginia.

Medieval

Anthology of Middle English Literature (1350–1485)
http://www.luminarium.org/medlit/
    Luminarium index site.

Bibliograpy of Spanish Comedias in English Translation, Part 1 of 2
ftp://listserv.ccit.arizona.edu/pub/listserv/comedia/biblio1.html
    Regular text bibliography from the University of Arizona.

**Labyrinth: Resources for Medieval Studies, The*
http://www.georgetown.edu/labyrinth/labyrinth-home.html
    Links to e-texts in many languages and to three major categories: national
    culture (Celtic, English, for example), international (manuscripts, sci-
    ence), and special topics (Arthurian studies, chivalry); much more; a
    Georgetown University site; reviewed in *Choice.*

medieval.ebbs.html
http://ebbs.english.vt.edu/medieval/medieval.ebbs.html
    Links to discussion list, texts from medieval period, databases (Chaucer
    Bibliography, Labyrinth), libraries, medieval sciences, and other pages.

Medieval Drama Links
http://www.leeds.ac.uk/theatre/emd/links.htm
    "Personal selection by Sydney Higgins," hosted by the Workshop The-
    atre of the University of Leeds; links to texts, costumes, music, medieval
    illustrations, and other theater pages.

Medieval English Drama
http://www.lib.rochester.edu/camelot/playbib.htm
    Unlinked bibliography in the series of Robbins Library (University of
    Rochester) bibliographies in medieval studies.

Medieval Sourcebook: Introduction
http://www.fordham.edu/halsall/sbook.html
    Links to selected sources, full text sources for medieval history (many
    early church documents), Saints' lives; part of the *Online Reference Book*
    for Medieval Studies; reviewed in *Choice.*

**Medieval Women*
http://www.millersv.edu/~english/homepage/duncan/medfem/medfem.html
    Quite beautiful, scrupulously prepared home page devoted to medieval
    women writers; composed by Bonnie Duncan, English Department of

Millersville University; divided into secular and religious writers, materials about women, secondary hypertexts by students, and more.

Middle English Collection at the Electronic Text Center, UVa
http://etext.virginia.edu/mideng.browse.html
Large list of e-texts (mostly from the Oxford Text Archive), most of which are publicly accessible; search engine.

Middle English Compendium
http://www.hti.umich.edu/mec/
Includes an enormous dictionary based on the print version; corpus of Middle English prose and verse; a hyperbibliography of Middle English prose and verse; multiple search options; by subscription only after January 1999.

***NetSERF: The Internet Connection for Medieval Resources*
http://www.wizard.net/~bharbin/netserf
Mega links site with connections to lists of links on medieval art, culture, drama, history, law, literature, philosophy, religion, and much more; sponsored by the Department of History at the Catholic University of America; reviewed in *Choice*.

Old English Pages
http://www.georgetown.edu/cball/oe/old_english.html
Encyclopedic compendium of resources for the study of Old English and Anglo-Saxon England, complete with links and search engines.

Online Medieval and Classical Library (DL SunSITE)
http://sunsite.berkeley.edu/OMACL/
Links page with connections to many e-texts and other sites connected to even more sites; unusually large list of authors with editions designated.

PLS Archive Gallery, The
http://www.epas.utoronto.ca/~medieval/www/pls/plsgall.html
Images of various modern productions of medieval English plays, including the York Cycle, the *Castle of Perseverance*, and *Gammer Gurton's Needle;* maintained by David Klausner at the University of Toronto.

Robbins Library Bibliographies
http://www.lib.rochester.edu/camelot/bibmenUniversityhtm
Webliography of medieval bibliographies (particularly for the Robin Hood Project and the Camelot Project) presented by the Robbins Library at the University of Rochester.

Women Writers of the Middle Ages
http://www.fordham.edu/halsall/med/womenbib.html
"Bibliography of Works by and about the Women of the Middle Ages"; a Robbins Library bibliography; not linked.

Renaissance and Seventeenth Century

Comedia Homepage
http://www.coh.arizona.edu/spanish/comedia/default.html
   Excellent site for the study of Hispanic classical theater; discussion groups;
   newsletters; links to texts in both Spanish and English; reviewed by
   Choice.

Early Modern Europe: Literature
http://history.hanover.edu/early/literatUniversityhtm
   A links-only page, emphasizing authors, mostly seventeenth and eighteenth century, although a few are later; produced by the History Department of Hanover College.

Early Modern Literary Studies: Home Page
http://www.humanities.ualberta.ca/emls/emlshome.html
   Refereed scholarly electronic journal examining English literature, literary culture, and language during the sixteenth and seventeenth centuries;
   sponsored by the University of Alberta.

English Literature: Early 17th Century (1603–1660)
http://www.luminarium.org/sevenlit/
   Index page from *Luminarium* site.

Essays and Articles on Sixteenth Century Renaissance English Literature
http://www.luminarium.org/renlit/essays.htm
   Luminarium selection of essays.

Renaissance Electronic Texts (RET) Main Page
http://library.utoronto.ca/www/utel/ret/ret.html
   Series of old-spelling, standardized markup language (SGML)–encoded
   editions of books and manuscripts from the English Renaissance; provided by the University of Toronto.

Renascence Editions: Works Printed in English 1477–1799
http://darkwing.uoregon.edu/~rbear/ren.htm
   Links page with an enormous list of e-texts, which are not represented as
   scholarly editions.

Sixteenth Century Renaissance English Literature (1485–1603)
http://www.luminarium.org/renlit/
   Luminarium index page; reviewed in *Choice*.

Some Concepts for Analyzing Renaissance Literature
http://www.apocalypse.org/pub/u/batalion/concepts.shtml
   Concepts, such as the Great Chain of Being, defined by Robert Evans
   of Auburn University; no links and no explanation of why the site was
   produced.

Eighteenth Century

American Literature (1700–1800): Reason and Revolution
http://falcon.jmUniversityedu/~ramseyil/amlitfirst.htm#F
   Part of the Internet School Library Media Center (ISLMC) site; primarily bibliographical with lists of links to authors and their works.

18th-Century English Literature—English Literature Net Links
http://englishlit.miningco.com/msub-18th.htm
   Commercial site that provides links to eighteenth century and the Restoration, resources, texts, archives; extremely detailed source on eighteenth-century literature and history.

18th Century Novel
http://miavx1.muohio.edu/~mandellc/novelcl.htm
   Part of a course site at Miami University, Ohio that provides syllabus information on the British novel and a couple of students' papers; links to the professor's handouts (British Liberalism, The Rise of the Novel).

18th Century Ring—Home Page
http://www.jaffebros.com/lee/18th/index.html
   Home page for a webring of WWW sites devoted to any and all aspects of the eighteenth century.

San Antonio College LitWeb Restoration and Eighteenth Century Literature Index
http://www.accd.edu/sac/english/bailey/18thcent.htm
   Part of the San Antonio College LitWeb maintained by Roger Bailey, Ph.D.; long list of author links and short list of eighteenth-century resources.

Nineteenth Century

American Literature—American Literary Classics—A Chapter A Day
http://www.americanliterature.com/
   Unusual literary site with a penchant for rare books and manuscripts; sponsored by the William Reese Company.

British Poetry 1780–1910: a Hypertext Archive of Scholarly Editions: Electronic Text Center
http://etext.lib.virginia.edu/britpo.html
   University of Virginia archive of works by various nineteenth-century authors (Coleridge, Hardy, Tennyson, for example); short list, with links to other e-text archives.

**Documenting the American South
http://sunsite.unc.edu/docsouth/

Focuses on Southern literature and history, particularly the nineteenth century; extensive e-text collection of slave narratives, first person narratives, and Southern literature.

Making of America

http://www.umdl.umich.edu/moa/

A digital library of 50,000 nineteenth-century American journals; sponsored by the University of Michigan and Cornell University.

**Romantic Chronology (Home Page)*

http://humanitas.ucsb.edu/projects/pack/rom-chrono/chrono.htm

Attractive, fully articulated website with authors and editors easily identifiable; beautiful images, reliable information, and thought-provoking essays; many links; reviewed in *Choice*.

**Romantic Circles*

http://www.inform.umd.edu/RC/

Unusually well-documented site with a band of collaborative authors, an advisory board, and an excellent selection of romantic sources; reviewed in *Choice*.

**Romanticism on the Net*

http://users.ox.ac.uk/~scat0385/

Peer-reviewed electronic journal devoted to romantic studies; indexed in MLA International Bibliography.

**Romanticism URL List*

http://www.muohio.edu/~mandellc/eng441/urllist.htm

Long, very helpful list of links, edited by Laura Mandell, English Department of Miami University, Ohio; provides a lot of guidance and explanation since it is designed for students.

**Victorian Web, The*

http://www.stg.brown.edu/projects/hypertext/landow/victorian/victov.html

Magnificent site conceived by George P. Landow, professor of English and art history at Brown University; a host of author pages linked to such categories as social context, economics, religion, and much more; reviewed in *Choice*.

**Victorian Women Writers Project, The*

http://www.indiana.edu/~letrs/vwwp/

Indiana University e-text project dedicated to Victorian women writers; works by many relatively obscure authors are already available; reviewed in *Choice*.

Women Romantic-Era Writers
http://orion.it.luc.edu/~acraciu/wrew.htm
> Page of links to dozens of sites concerning women writers of the nineteenth century; maintained by Adriana Craciun, English Department, Loyola University.

YPN: Arts & Literature: Literature: Poetry: Romantics & Others
http://ypn.netresponse.com/DOCS/5339.html
> Small selection of links to romantic poetry sites, all reviewed by an unidentified smart aleck; some of the links no longer work; valuable as a good example of something bad about Internet literary pages.

Twentieth Century

Éclat: The "Essential" Comparative Literature and Theory Site
http://ccat.sas.upenn.edu/Complit/Eclat/
> Large, elaborate site maintained by the Comparative Literature Department at the University of Pennsylvania; hundreds of literary links; reviewed in *Choice*.

GBK 491—The Modern Temper: Visions and Revisions
http://www.athens.net/~lnoles/gbk/gbk491.html
> Modernist readings in literature and philosophy from an assortment in the Great Books Program that originated at Mercer University.

**Index of Web Sites on Modernism, An
http://www.modcult.brown.edu/people/Scholes/modlist/Title.html
> Annotated index of links maintained by the Malcolm S. Forbes Center at Brown University; extensive and useful.

Literary Kicks
http://www.charm.net/~brooklyn/litkicks.html
> A Beat poets fan page.

**Literature and Culture of the American 1950s
http://dept.english.upenn.edu/~afilreis/50s/home.html
> Elaborate, fascinating page of interdisciplinary links for an advanced English class at the University of Pennsylvania; model for course-related website; reviewed by *Choice*.

Poems Poetry Poets
http://www.execpc.com/~jon/
> Poetry links page by an ardent fan named (apparently) John Faragher; emphasis on poetry of Wisconsin, among other major obscurities; very interesting, quirky browsing site.

Poetry Cafe: Main Entrance to Contemporary Poetry
http://www.poetrycafe.com/

Colorful (distracting) commercial site with many links to poetry, multimedia, and various obscure contemporary writers.

**Postcolonial and Postimperial Literature: An Overview
http://www.stg.brown.edu/projects/hypertext/landow/post/misc/postov.html
Large, elaborate, and unique; pages devoted to countries, authors, bibliography, postcolonial theory, and much more; created by George P. Landow, author of the *Victorian Web;* part of Brown University's Internet offerings; still under construction; reviewed in *Choice.*

Ethnic Literatures

African American Literature
http://www.usc.edu/Library/Ref/Ethnic/black_lit_main.html
Provides a short history of Black literature; links to sources for literary criticism, African-American poets, poetry, drama, novels, novelists, and short fiction.

American Studies, Black History and Literature
http://www.keele.ac.uk/depts/as/Literature/amlit.black.html
Explores African-American presence in literature and history from various aspects; links to texts and resources occupy most of the page; historical texts and links to the other sources are offered at the end.

Andrew Crumey's "Scottish Writers"
http://www.geocities.com/Athens/Acropolis/9172/scot.html
Fan site of Scottish literature links.

Asian and Asian-American Poets
http://www.rothpoem.com/asiapoet.html
Commercial publisher's site with a list of Asian and Asian-American poets and biographical information on two of them: Carolyn Lau and Timothy Liu; no actual poems, only titles.

Canadian Literature Archive
http://canlit.st-john.umanitoba.ca/Canlitx/Canlit_homepage.html
Information on Canadian writers, literary organizations, texts, Canadian library archives, bibliographies and biographies; searching the page is somewhat difficult; reviewed by *Choice.*

CWIS Listings
http://www.georgetown.edu/tamlit/cwis/cwis.html
Index of Campus Wide Information Servers in American literature and related fields; page devoted to links for African-American, Asian-American, and Chicano studies.

Epistrophy: The Jazz Literature Archive
http://ie.uwindsor.ca/jazz/

Collection of twentieth-century texts concerning or influenced by jazz; includes poetry by Langston Hughes.

Index of Native American Authors Online
http://hanksville.phast.umass.edu/poems/poets/index.cgi
Brief list of links to Native American authors characterized as story-tellers; reviewed by *Choice*.

Local Color Fiction and Regionalism: Selected Bibliography
http://www.gonzaga.edu/faculty/campbell/enl311/regbib.htm
Constantly updated bibliography; links to MLA Citation Format and Project Muse.

Native American Authors
http://www.ipl.org/ref/native/
Information on Native American authors; bibliographies, biographies, and links to online resources (interviews, online texts, tribal websites); index is searchable by author, title, and tribe; reviewed in *Choice*.

OzLit Vicnet—Australian Books, Australian Literature
http://home.vicnet.net.au/~ozlit/index.html
Rich source on Australian literature; links to writers, books, literature, news, online e-zine, literary sites, newspapers, and so forth; constantly updated and expanding.

Poetry and Prose of the Harlem Renaissance
http://www.nkUniversityedu/~diesmanj/poetryindex.html
Full e-text versions of many Harlem Renaissance authors; entries are liable to disappear (as Langston Hughes corpus already has) because of copyright infringements.

UGA African American Studies
http://www.uga.edu/~iaas/History.html
Brief biographical sketches of the most significant African Americans in history and literature; key figures are organized in chronological order, starting with Benjamin Banneker and ending with Cynthia A. McKinney; bibliography included.

Women and Literature

Celebration of Women Writers, A
http://www.cs.cmUniversityedu/afs/cs.cmUniversityedu/user/mmbt/
www/women/celebration.html
Developed in association with the On-Line Books Page; contributions of women writers throughout history, with easy access to online information; many, many links.

Diotima: Women & Gender in the Ancient World
http://www.uky.edu/ArtsSciences/Classics/gender.html
>   Reviewed in *Choice*.

Orlando Project, The
http://www.ualberta.ca/ORLANDO/
>   Site that claims to be "writing the first full scholarly history of women's writing in the British Isles": an electronic project based at the University of Alberta.

Voices from the Gaps: Women Writers of Color
http://english.cla.umn.edu/lkd/vfg/vfghome
>   Pages on individual authors, arranged by name, birthday, birthplace, ethnic group, or significant dates; discussion room and related sites; located at the University of Minnesota; reviewed (not favorably) by *Choice*.

Women in Literature—A Literary Overview
http://www.stg.brown.edu/projects/hypertext/landow/victorian/gender/
womlitov.html
>   Part of the *Victorian Web* essay by Elizabeth Lee, senior at Brown University, on the critical thinking of Elaine Showalter; links to the Brontes, Elizabeth Gaskell, and Elizabeth Browning, among others.

Women Romantic-Era Writers
http://orion.it.luc.edu/~acraciu/wrew.htm
>   Page of links to dozens of sites concerning women writers of the nineteenth century; maintained by Adriana Craciun, English Department, Loyola University.

Women Writers Project
http://www.stg.brown.edu/projects/wwp/wwp_home.html
>   Site designed to "make accessible a state-of the-art electronic textbase of women's writing in English before 1830"; sponsored by Brown University.

Women's Studies: A Research Guide
http://www.nypl.org/research/chss/grd/resguides/women.html
>   Guide to research in the New York Public Library, one of the most important resource centers for women's studies in the United States; reviewed in *Choice*.

3. E-TEXTS ARCHIVES

American Literature: Electronic Texts
http://www.keele.ac.uk/depts/as/Literature/amlit.html
>   General index to virtual libraries of American literature, including twentieth-century texts; links to other American literature websites, teaching resources, Canadian literature, and more.

American Verse Project
http://www.hti.umich.edu/english/amverse/
> Electronic archive of volumes of American poetry prior to 1920; available in HTML and SGML; part of the Humanities Text Initiative at the University of Michigan.

Banned Books On-Line
http://www.cs.cmUniversityedu/People/spok/banned-books.html
> History of censorship and works that have been censored; links to censored authors and texts.

Books.com
http://www.books.com/scripts/lib.exe
> Short index page offers only two options: browsing the electronic library and visiting it via FTP; great variety and number of sources.

Books On-Line, New Listings
http://www.cs.cmUniversityedu/booknew.html
> Contains a large list of links to works that have recently been added to the site's online library (*The Canterbury Tales*, Lewis Carroll, and many more).

British Poetry 1780–1910: A Hypertext Archive of Scholarly Editions: Electronic Text Center
http://etext.lib.virginia.edu/britpo.html
> University of Virginia archive of works of various authors (Coleridge, Hardy, Tennyson, Rossetti, for example).

CELT: Corpus of Electronic Texts (Home Page)
http://www.ucc.ie/celt/index.html
> Online resource for historical and contemporary Irish documents, including literature, his-tory, and politics.

Christian Classics Ethereal Library
http://ccel.wheaton.edu/
> Large index to religious nonfiction, fiction, hymns, and reference sources; arranged in alphabetical order; an easily accessible source to a wide range of e-texts.

Classics at the Online Literature Library
http://www.literature.org/Works/
> Links to e-text versions of works by famous authors.

Digital Collections (DL SunSITE)
http://sunsite.berkeley.edu/Collections/
> Links page to the impressive digital collection developed by the University of California at Berkeley and Sun Microsystems; links to some image sources, literature, the *Online Medieval and Classical Library* (huge

source), nineteenth-century literature, and so forth; contains both specialized links and broader connections.

Digital Library Federation Home Page
http://lcweb.loc.gov/loc/ndlf/
Collection of digital materials, available to students and scholars; index page with links to organization information and to reference materials and publications.

Douglass—Archives of American Public Address
http://douglass.speech.nwUniversityedu/
Part of an electronic archive of American oratory and related documents for general scholarship and courses in American rhetorical history at Northwestern; reviewed in *Choice*.

Electronic Poetry Center Home Page
http://wings.buffalo.edu/epc/
Site emphasizing contemporary poetry and small presses; sponsored by the State University of New York at Buffalo.

Electronic Text Center—University of Virginia
http://etext.lib.virginia.edu/
Online archive of thousands of SGML-encoded e-texts and images and a library service offering hardware and software suitable for creation and analysis of text; especially strong in American letters.

Electronic Texts
http://odin.english.udel.edu/dean/etexts.html
Offers links to texts in Middle English, Dante sources, Boccaccio studies, texts in Latin, and indexes and bibliographies; electronic bulletin information and lectures.

Great Books Index
http://books.mirror.org/
Index to Great Books in Translation with links to online editions where available.

***Index of Poets in Representative Poetry On-Line, An*
http://library.utoronto.ca/www/utel/rp/indexauthors.html
Enormous index to poetry in the extensive e-text collection edited by the English Department of the University of Toronto; invaluable for pre-twentieth-century works.

Internet Classics Archive: 441 Searchable Works of Classical Literature
http://classics.mit.edu/index.html
User-friendly site with access to e-texts of classical literature, other sources, and a trivia game; help pages with answers to most frequently asked questions; option to purchase books and materials.

On-Line Books Page, The
http://www.cs.cmUniversityedu/books.html
> Searchable archive with over 7,000 listings, authors, titles, and subjects; includes features such as "A Celebration of Women Writers" and "Banned Books On-Line"; constantly updated and growing.

Online Medieval and Classical Library (DL SunSITE), The
http://sunsite.berkeley.edu/OMACL/
> Page of links to a vast range of individual classical and medieval e-texts; links to other enormous lists; search engine.

Oxford Text Archive, The
http://firth.natcorp.ox.ac.uk/ota/public/index.shtml
> Archive of over 2,500 e-texts in HTML and SGML with full-text search option; up-to-date materials; advanced catalog with easy research options and other resources.

Project Bartleby Archive
http://www.cc.columbia.edu/acis/bartleby/
> Archive containing e-texts, mostly from the nineteenth and twentieth centuries; search engine.

Project Gutenberg
http://www.gutenberg.net/
> Extensive collection of e-texts of (mostly) public domain works, some 1,596 of them at last count, a few of which are copyrighted; texts are presented in very basic format, and errors are tolerated; a large list of links to other e-text sites is classified according to how they are organized, around an author, work, theme, and so forth; latest additions include works by Jack London, O. Henry, Andrew Lang, Mary Roberts Rinehart, Christopher Marlowe, Wilkie Collins, and Plato.

4. LITERARY CRITICS, CRITICISM, THEORIES, AND THEORISTS

Colonialism, Postcolonialism, and Literature: Theorists and Critics
http://www.stg.brown.edu/projects/hypertext/landow/post/poldiscourse/theorists.html
> Index of critics; biographical information; some excerpted texts and bibliographies.

**Johns Hopkins Guide Literary Theory and Criticism, The
http://www.press.jhUniversityedu/books/hopkins_guide_to_literary_theory/
> Large, elaborate, subscrition site devoted to literary theory and criticism of all sorts from many periods; fifteen entries are freely available for demonstration purposes; reviewed in *Choice*.

Postmodern Criticism

http://www.geocities.com/Athens/Acropolis/2209/pomo.html

> Large list of links to resources on criticism (encyclopedia sources, e-zines, studies); also a list of critics with links to their works.

Postmodern Thought

http://www.cudenver.edu/~mryder/itc_data/postmodern.html/

> Part of an academic page sponsored by the University of Colorado; links to resources, readings, and critics (Barthes, Derrida, Baudrillard, and so forth); a large, reliable, useful source with plenty of information and a search engine.

5. GENERAL GUIDES, LISTS, AND INDICES

Subject Directories

Access to Internet and Subject Resources: Alphabetical

http://www2.lib.udel.edu/subj/

> Alphabetical subject tree of discipline-related sites maintained by the University of Delaware Library.

AlphaSearch—Gateway to the "Academic" Web

http://www.calvin.edu/library/as/

> Gateway site to academic websites; search engine; maintained by the library of Calvin College Theological Seminary.

American Studies Web

http://www.georgetown.edu/crossroads/asw/

> Provides reference and research possibilities in economy and politics, race and ethnicity, gender and sexuality, literature and hypertext, performance and broadcasting, and so forth; search engine.

**Argus Clearinghouse

http://www.clearinghouse.net/index.html

> Subject tree; general guide to academic sources on Internet with enormous lists of rated links.

Arts and Humanities

http://galaxy.einet.net/GJ/arts.html

> Variety of links: music, arts, and humanities collections; e-journals and film resources; links are academic (University of California, Texas A & M University) and institutional (Library of Congress).

**Britannica Internet guide

http://www.ebig.com/

> Ongoing collection of reviews for Internet sites in a subject tree format with a convenient rating system; reviewed in *Choice*.

BUBL LINK: LIbraries of Networked Knowledge
http://bubl.ac.uk/link/
> Combination search engine (with LINK) and browser (by Dewey class, by subject, and at random); maintained by the Andersonian Library, Strathclyde University, Glasgow, Scotland.

Cultural Treasures of the Internet
http://shirley.cs.widener.edu/clark/clark.html
> Enormous index to almost everything, from aesthetics, book reviews, education to linguistics, human rights, and women's studies; really useful source for broad research.

Daedalus's Guide to the Web
http://www.georgetown.edu/labyrinth/general/general.html
> Provides starting assistance for many kinds of research; links to net directories, libraries, and universities; information on citing e-sources and copyright issues.

EDSITEment
http://edsitement.neh.gov/
> Entry to website with links to forty-nine top humanities sites, lesson plans, and in-school activities; jointly sponsored by the National Endowment for the Humanities, among others.

GeoCities—The Largest Community on the Web!
http://www.geocities.com/
> General subject tree site, with arts and literature one of the branches.

ICOM Welcome Page
http://www.icom.org/
> International Council of Museums home page offers information on this council and their policies; their virtual library links to virtually every subject, including literature; resource links are not separated from the council information.

Indexes, Abstracts, Bibliographies, and Table of Contents Services
http://info.lib.uh.edu/indexes/indexes.htm
> Easy-to-search site, separated into three main directories: art and humanities, science and technology, and social sciences; humanities directory has links to history, art, music, but not (yet) to literature and theater; reviewed in *Choice*.

INFOMINE: Scholarly Internet Resource Collections
http://lib-www.ucr.edu/
> University of California academic subject tree with search engine.

IPL Reference Center
http://ipl.si.umich.edu/ref/
   Internet public library site to answer reference questions in most academic areas.

Librarian's Guide to the Best Information on the Net
http://www.saUniversityedu/CWIS/Internet/Wild/index.htm
   Sites chosen by librarians at O'Keefe Library, St. Ambrose University;
   very lengthy lists of links in all academic subjects; reviewed by *Choice.*

Librarians' Index to the Internet
http://sunsite.berkeley.edu/internetindex/
   Search engine and subject tree prepared by University of California at
   Berkeley librarians with an emphasis on new sites.

Lycos Top 5%
http://point.lycos.com/categories/
   Subject tree leading to rated sites in conjunction with the *Lycos* search
   engine; it is called the best of the web, but it has only limited academic
   use since all categories of Internet subjects are included.

Magellan
http://www.mckinley.com/
   Yet another search engine and subject tree, covering all subjects (nonacademic and academic) with an option to search reviewed sites only.

Malaspina Great Books Home Page—Five Star Sites
http://www.mala.bc.ca/~mcneil/fivestar.htm
   Very large list of literary and cultural sites that have been awarded a five-
   star rating by *Malaspina Great Books:* an interdisciplinary site maintained by Russell McNeill.

Mining Co., The
http://home.miningco.com/
   Enormous subject tree with many categories and subcategories eventuat-
   ing in lists of annotated and informally rated websites.

Resources of Scholarly Societies by Subject
http://www.lib.uwaterloo.ca/society/subjects_soc.html
   Large list of directories ranging from agriculture to women's issue; list
   leads to even larger groups of links; URL stability index is included to in-
   form users of URL changes.

Scout Report Signpost
http://www.signpost.org/signpost/
   Site for searching "only the best Internet resources, as chosen by the

editorial staff of the Scout Report"; user may choose brief summaries or a long format.

Search the Gateway to the Internet
http://www.lib.uiowa.edu/gw/keyword.html#subject
Subject tree (academic subjects) and search engine from the University of Iowa.

**Voice of the Shuttle: Web Page for Humanities Research*
http://humanitas.ucsb.edu/
Invaluable subject tree compiled by Alan Liu of the English Department of the University of California at Santa Barbara; includes separate guides for English literature, other literature, and literary theory; most categories are unannotated, but some very sparse annotations appear toward the ends of branches on the subject tree; reviewed in *Choice*.

**World Lecture Hall*
http://www.utexas.edu/world/lecture/
"Links to pages created by faculty worldwide who are using the Web to deliver class materials"; virtually all academic disciplines represented; maintained by the University of Texas; search engine; reviewed in *Choice*.

WWW Virtual Library
http://vlib.stanford.edu/Overview.html
Big subject tree with academic categories.

Yahoo! Arts:Humanities:Literature
http://www.yahoo.com/Arts/Humanities/Literature/
Very popular subject tree search engine.

Academic Resources: Universities and Libraries

American Universities
http://www.clas.ufl.edu/CLAS/american-universities.html
Large alphabetical list of links to American universities and colleges and their respective home pages.

Bodleian Library WWW Server—Towards an Image Catalogue
http://rsl.ox.ac.uk/imacat.html
Offers images (Marguerite de Navarre, Hezekiah, anatomical images) in both graphics interchange format (GIF) and joint photographic experts group (JPEG) format.

Braintrack—University Index
http://www.braintrack.com
Immense linked list of universities and colleges, sorted by continent and nation.

Hutchins Library—Electronic Resources
http://www.berea.edu/library/libindex.html
> Links to multiple indexes and periodicals that cover virtually every aspect of research; some of the indexes are general (ProQuest), whereas others are specialized in certain areas (agriculture, literature, medicine); links have explanations.

**Library of Congress Home Page
http://lcweb.loc.gov/
> Links to enormous Library of Congress catalogs and library services online; excellent, reliable source for researchers, librarians, and scholars.

Libraries on the Web: USA—Academic
http://sunsite.Berkeley.EDU/Libweb/usa-acad.html
> Entryway to a vast linked list of academic libraries in the United States.

Libweb—Library WWW Servers
http://sunsite.berkeley.edu/Libweb/
> Links to over 2,400 pages from libraries in over seventy countries.

**National library catalogues worldwide
http://www.library.uq.edUniversityau/ssah/jeast/
> Links maintained by the University of Queensland Library; contains all the information needed to connect to national libraries around the world; reviewed in *Choice.*

Online Publications (about Internet Resources)

Hersh Web Site Observer OnLine
http://www.webpan.com/aeh/thwso/
> Commercial newsletter that reviews new websites; extensive archives of earlier issues; searchable, but literary sites are not emphasized.

Internet Resources Newsletter
http://www.hw.ac.uk/libWWW/irn/irn.html
> Free newletter reviewing websites for academics, published by the Internet Resources Centre at Heriot-Watt University in the United Kingdom; literary sites are included but certainly not emphasized.

Netsurfer Digest Home Page
http://www.netsurf.com/nsd/index.html
> Free e-zine that supplies weekly links to "a selection of neat online sites."

Word, Literature, Journals, Books, The
http://www.speakeasy.org/~dbrick/Hot/word.html
> Large list of links to reference works, online books and bookstores, online journals and magazines, poetry, and much more.

Books

***Amazon.com Books! Earth's Biggest Bookstore*
http://www.amazon.com/exec/obidos/subst/index2.html/
7752-6366591-486492
>   Commercial site offering books from a stock of more than three million
>   titles; great variety with (mostly) low prices; publishing news, book re-
>   views (by readers and even by authors themselves), images, and search
>   engines.

Bibliomania, The Network Library: Home Page
http://www.bibliomania.com/
>   Search engine and links for books in many categories; connected to
>   *BookPages*, "your British bookseller."

Book Lovers: Fine Books and Literature
http://www.xs4all.nl/~pwessel/
>   Excellent source on a wide variety of literature components; links to rare
>   books (the study of book history), general sites (starting point), book-
>   sellers and publishers, libraries and collections, literary journals, writers
>   and poets, and so forth.

Book Nook
http://www.jps.net/gmreed/lit/lit.htm
>   Fan site with brief descriptions of multicultural works: African American,
>   Mexican American, Asian American, Native American, Jewish American.

Books
http://www.cis.ohio-state.edu:80/hypertext/faq/usenet/books/top.html
>   Contains links to the Bible, book clubs, Arthurian booklist (from Usenet),
>   and frequently asked questions on libraries and authors; most of the in-
>   formation is from various Usenet sources.

Books On-Line: Authors
http://www.cs.cmUniversityedu/bookauthors.html
>   Search engine for authors online.

bookstore.com
http://www.bookstore.com/forauth.html
>   Exhaustive list of authors whose works have been translated into English;
>   searchable; part of an Internet bookstore site: "A Clean Well-Lighted
>   Place for Books."

BookWeb: Home Page
http://ambook.org/
>   Online bookstore, with book news, book events, a searchable database of
>   bookstores and home pages, book-selling statistics, links to book-related
>   websites, and an entertainment corner.

**BookWire*
http://www.bookwire.com/
>   Commercial site that offers purchasing of books and materials as well as
>   reviews of current publications and bestsellers, literary features, and
>   publishing news; *Bookwire* index provides access to more than 7,000 in-
>   dustry-related websites (authors, works).

Internet Book Information Center, The (IBIC)
http://sunsite.unc.edu/ibic/IBIC-homepage.html
>   Extremely large source offering a guide to book-related issues, links to e-
>   zines and e-texts, ordering information, various search engines, links to
>   usenet newsgroups, and world literature hypermail archive.

Mystery Writers of America
http://www.bookwire.com/mwa/
>   Unabashed commercial site with interesting genre, publishing, and orga-
>   nizational links.

Write Page, The
http://www.writepage.com/
>   Online newsletter with over 300 pages of author and book information;
>   links to children's books, fantasy, serious fiction, romance, westerns, and
>   online writing; every link is accompanied by a short description.

Discussion Groups: E-Mail and Usenet

Directory of Scholarly and Professional E-Conferences
http://www.n2h2.com/KOVACS/
>   Links to e-conferences by subject or category listing and alphabetical
>   listing; link to gopher source.

Internet Mailing Lists Guides and Resources
http://www.nlc-bnc.ca/ifla/I/training/listserv/lists.htm
>   Provides some technical information on list servers, explaining their pur-
>   pose and possibilities; addresses to particular list servers are offered;
>   source is too general for a specific search.

Liszt, the Mailing List Directory
http://www.liszt.com/
>   Search engine has the capacity to search over 84,000 mailing lists of
>   the main directory; sections include business, education, religion, and
>   humanities.

Publicly Accessible Mailing Lists
http://www.neosoft.com/internet/paml/
>   Information about public mailing lists, subscribing, and list resources
>   and compilations.

tile.net
http://www.tile.net/
>   Comprehensive Internet reference site with links to discussion lists, Usenet newsgroups, FTP site, computer products vendors, and Internet and web design companies.

6. INSTITUTIONS

AHDS: Homepage
http://ahds.ac.uk/
>   Arts and Humanities Data Service (AHDS) provides links to collections, publications, and information on user support and training; separate directories (history, archaeology, Oxford Text Archive) offer further information; a British academic home page.

American Arts and Letters Network
http://www.aaln.org/
>   Page with database containing links to over 600 resources in the arts and humanities; special features (that is, site of the week) option; search engines and browser; information on teaching and technology.

American Council of Learned Societies (non-JS), The
http://www.acls.org/
>   Private nonprofit organization whose goal is to "advance humanistic studies"; links to fellowship and grant programs, publications, online scholarly resources, and so forth; this society also has its own news and events information.

American Studies Crossroads Project
http: //www.georgetown.edu/crossroads/
>   Sponsored by the American Studies Association; annotated bibliography of course materials and syllabi; information about technology and teaching workshops.

Association for Computers and the Humanities
http://www.ach.org/
>   International professional organization serving people who work closely with computer-aided research in language and literature studies and other humanity fields; links to society events, publications, and e-sources.

Brown University Scholarly Technology Group
http://www.stg.brown.edu/
>   A center that supports the development and use of information technology in research and teaching, focusing on hypertext, SGML, networked communication and publishing, and electronic learning.

CETH: Center for Electronic Texts in the Humanities
http://www.ceth.rutgers.edu/
>   Provides information about electronic text creation and use for scholars, plus a guide to evaluating literary etexts.

CH Working Papers
http://www.chass.utoronto.ca/epc/chwp/
>   Devoted to computer-assisted research; papers and essays on the sociology of computer-based research and other publications; most articles are refereed; entries are in both English and French.

CHASS Facility, University of Toronto
http://datacentre.chass.utoronto.ca/
>   CHASS is a computing facility within the Faculty of Arts and Science at the University of Toronto; promotes computing in research and teaching; the page, which should be useful for teachers, offers software, tutorials, user information, frequently asked questions, and so forth.

Folger Shakespeare Library, The
http://www.folger.edu/
>   Attractive site with listings of public events, academic resources, and general information related to the Folger Shakespeare Library.

Humanist Discussion Group
http://www.princeton.edu/~mccarty/humanist/
>   Information on an international electronic seminar ("Humanist") whose goal is connecting humanities with technology, a forum for academic, "intellectual, scholarly, pedagogical" discussion; links lead to some volumes of *Humanist*.

Humanities Text Initiative
http://www.umich.edu/
>   Umbrella organization for acquisition, creation, and maintenance of electronic texts, primarily in SGML, but with HTML viewing options.

Institute for Advanced Technology in the Humanities
http://jefferson.village.virginia.edu/
>   A center at the University of Virginia dedicated to exploring and expanding the use of technology in humanities research; supports major scholarly projects such as Rossetti, Blake, Dickinson, and Whitman projects, many historical projects, and the electronic journal, *Postmodern Culture*.

MHRA's Home Page
http://www.lib.cam.ac.uk/MHRA/
>   Information about the Modern Humanities Research Association at Cambridge University.

Michigan Hemingway Society: Goals and Objectives
http://www.freeway.net/community/civic/hemingway/hemgoals.html
> Straightforward promotion for the society—which is at least as interested in Michigan as in Hemingway.

National Archives and Records Administration
http://www.nara.gov/
> Research page; links to genealogy, historical records, four research tools (such as Archival Information Locator), current government information, and professional services (grants, employment).

National Council of Teachers of English—Welcome!
http://www.ncte.org/
> Home page for the National Council of Teachers of English (NCTE) with links, mostly professional and pedagogical.

National Endowment for the Humanities, The
http://www.neh.gov/
> Home page with guidelines for grant applications, links to information about NEH-funded activities all over the country, exhibition schedules, and a useful list of NEH-sponsored websites, many of which are literary.

National Geographic
http://www.nationalgeographic.com/main.html
> Commercial site offering previews of *National Geographic* magazine, a discussion forum, and book and materials ordering information.

National Writing Centers Association Page, The
http://departments.colgate.edu/diw/NWCA.html
> Links to writing center resources, tutor stories, centers online, resources for writers, and writing center start-up kit; excellent source for help in proofreading and editing; for both beginners and more advanced writers.

Nobel Prize Internet Archive, The
http://www.nobelprizes.com/
> Searchable site with information about all Nobel Prize winners.

Pulitzer Prize—Archive
http://www.pulitzer.org/archive/
> Time line of past winners; more nearly complete information about winners of the past three years.

Smithsonian Institution Home Page, The
http://www.si.edu/
> Visually rich source with many images and a wide range of information; search engines provide fast access to resources: *Encyclopedia Smithsonian, Smithsonian Magazine,* online research information system, and so forth.

7. INTERNET

Evaluating Internet Resources
http://www.albany.edu/library/internet/evaluate.html
    Prescribes evaluation standards for Internet sources with suggestions for
    what elements of a particular page to note.

Evaluating Web Resources
http: //www.science.widener.edu/~withers/webeval.htm
    Extensive site developed by the librarians at Widener University's Wof-
    gram Memorial Library.

hypertext: renaissance
http://www.artsci.wustl.edu/~jntolva/
    Excellent source for teachers and instructors; contains teaching tools
    connected with web tools; most of the programs (creative writing, me-
    dieval literature) are written in JavaScript.

Impact of Electronic Journals on Scholarly Communication:
A Citation Analysis
http://info.lib.uh.edu/pr/v7/n5/hart7n5.html
    Refereed article focusing on issues involving scholarly research and
    electronic resources; very long text with no links.

Internet Citation Guide
http://www.stedwards.edu/cfpages/stoll/internet.htm
    Suggestions for Internet citation, but format is not MLA; instructions for
    bibliographical citations, footnote and endnote citations, and informa-
    tion on additional sources about citing; created in 1995.

Internet News, The
http://www.interport.net/interport/news_top_page.html
    Page describing some of the terminology of the Internet, including suf-
    fixes, such as .alt, .biz, .talk, and so forth; examples of certain Internet
    groups.

Internet Public Library, The
http://www.ipl.org/
    Links to *Online Literary Criticism Collection* (over 1,200 critical and bi-
    ographical sites), collections (newspapers, magazines, e-texts, and so
    forth), and some information about the page.

Internet Resources Meta-Index
http://www.ncsa.uiuc.edu/SDG/Software/Mosaic/MetaIndex.html
    Solely links to a wide range of sites on the net, including WWW, gophers,
    telnet sources and FTP servers.

Internet Resources: Internet Lists
http://www.mcs.brandonUniversityca/~ennsnr/Resources/lists.html

List of Internet resources lists: dozens of them, with a primitive, comic book rating system consisting of "wow" printed in yellow next to the (presumably) superior lists.

Learn the Net: An Internet Guide and Tutorial
http://www.learnthenet.com/english/index.html
Introductory, commercial guide to the Internet; links to using Internet in educational surroundings.

SGML/XML Web Page-Home, The
http://www.sil.org/sgml/sgml.html
Information on the use of computer software and languages; extensive bibliography and technical support data.

TACT Web 1.0 Demonstration Server
http://tactweb.mcmaster.ca/
Guide to and demonstration of text analysis computer tools (TACTs) that allow sophisticated searches and analyses of electronic text accessed on the web.

Text Encoding Initiative Home Page
http://www.uic.edu/orgs/tei/
Product of an organization that is developing guidelines for the preparation of e-texts for scholarly research; links to a short description of the organization, archives, tutorials, bulletin boards, resources, and so forth; updated regularly.

CHAPTER 5

Literary Guide to the Internet:
A Bibliography (Continued)

8. AUTHORS AND ANONYMOUS WORKS

Achebe, Chinua

ComL100: Resources—Chinua Achebe
http://ccat.sas.upenn.edu/Complit/coml100/achebe/
> Course-related site at the University of Pennsylvania with a variety of useful links to African sources and Achebe's work, including lectures and public appearances.

Aeschylus

Aeschylus (ca. 525–456 B.C.)
http://www.mala.bc.ca/~mcneil/aesch.htm
> *Malaspina Great Books* links page.

Perseus Encyclopedia Aeschylus
http://hydra.perseus.tufts.edu/cgi-bin/text?lookup=encyclopedia+Aeschylus
> Part of the Perseus Project at Tufts University; numerous links within the *Perseus Encyclopedia* and to e-texts.

Albee, Edward

EducETH—Albee, Edward
http://educeth.ethz.ch/english/readinglist/albee,edward.html#virginiawoolf
> Part of *EducEth English* page; links to biography and other resources; a synopsis of *Who's Afraid of Virginia Woolf?;* comments by teachers and students; teaching tips.

Ancrene Riwle

Encyclopedia.com—Results for Ancren Riwle
http://www.encyclopedia.com/articles/
> *Concise Columbia Electronic Encyclopedia* entry with a few links to other relative entries within the site.

Religious Justification . . .
http://www.total.net/~tritton/riwle.html
> Rather impassioned student response to having read the *Ancrene Riwle* for a course.

Anderson, Sherwood

Sherwood Anderson Links
http://www.nwohio.com/clydeoh/sherwood.htm
> Primarily a tourist site, with emphasis on Anderson's hometown in Ohio; several more literary links; sponsored by the Internet bookstore *Amazon. com.*

Aristophanes

Classic Text, The: Aristophanes
http://www.uwm.edu/Dept/Library/special/exhibits/clastext/clspg033.htm
> Part of an ambitious exhibit of published texts with images and commentary; links to similar sites for world-famous authors, mostly classical.

Aristotle

"Poetics" by Aristotle
http://www.csulb.edu/~jvancamp/361r12.html
> Translation of Aristotle's work by S. H. Butcher with discussion questions and bibliography.

Arnold, Matthew

Poetry Archives—Matthew Arnold 1822–1888
http://library.advanced.org/3247/cgi-bin/dispover.cgi?frame=none&poet=arnold.matthew
> Page devoted to Arnold's poetry and prose (e-texts) and to biographical information; links to other websites on the same subject, bibliography, and so forth.

Atwood, Margaret

Atwood Society Margaret Atwood Information Site
http://www.cariboo.bc.ca/atwood/
> Active, current home page with links to Atwood's works, bibliography, publications about her, and Atwood society news.

Margaret Atwood (1939–)
http://www.mala.bc.ca/~mcneil/atwood.htm
   Malaspina Great Books links page.

Auden, W. H.

W. H. Auden Society, The
http://www.columbia.edu/~em36/audensociety/
   Pages devoted to the society's business and to various Auden texts and
   scholarly notes about his work.

Augustine

Classic Text, The: St. Augustine
http://www.uwm.edu/Dept/Library/special/exhibits/clastext/clspg059.htm
   Part of a beautiful site inspired by an exhibit of textual editions, emphasizing classical authors.

St. Augustine (354–430)
http://www.mala.bc.ca/~mcneil/august.htm
   Malaspina Great Books links page.

Austen, Jane

Jane Austen (1775–1817)
http://www.mala.bc.ca/~mcneil/austen.htm
   Malaspina Great Books links page.

**Republic of Pemberley
http://www.pemberley.com/
   Fan site operated by a volunteer committee; links to discussion groups,
   e-texts, bibliography, biography, academic articles, other fan sites, and
   so forth; search device by keyword; Jane Austen Information Page has a
   staggering number of links.

Bacon, Francis

Essays of Francis Bacon (1601), The
http://ourworld.compuserve.com/homepages/mike_donnelly/bacon.htm
   E-text versions of Bacon's essays with a page of links; glossary of ar-
   chaic words and phrases.

Baldwin, James

James Baldwin
http://www.geocities.com/SoHo/Lofts/6918/
   "(Some of) the life and (most of) the works of James Baldwin," according to the unidentified author of this GeoCities site; brief biography and
   list of works with no links.

Balzac, Honoré de

Honoré de Balzac (1799–1850)
http://members.aol.com/balssa/balzac/balzac.html
Introductory page with portrait by Louis Boulanger and notes; links to other pages about Balzac (his works, other portraits, bibliography, webliography).

Baudelaire, Charles

Charles Baudelaire
http://www.tardis.ed.ac.uk/~angus/Poetry/Poems/c_baudelaire.html
Part of Angus McIntyre's personal page; three poems by Baudelaire; links to home page and a few other poems.

Beckett, Samuel

Samuel Beckett (1906–1989)
http://www.mala.bc.ca/~mcneil/beckett.htm
Malaspina Great Books links page.

Samuel Beckett Resources and Links
http://www.geocities.com/HotSprings/5518/Beck_Links.html
Huge page of links to sites about Beckett, sponsored by GeoCities; links to the *New York Times,* the *New York Review of Books,* Beckett, interviews, e-texts, online bookstores, videos, audios, festivals, and net search.

Bede, The Venerable

Catholic Encyclopedia: The Venerable Bede
http://www.knight.org/advent/cathen/02384a.htm
Part of the New Advent's page; a Catholic website; biographical information.

Behn, Aphra

Aphra Behn Page
http://ourworld.compuserve.com/homepages/r_nestvold/
Biography and links, both specific to the author and general to her period; part of the *Baroque Ring.*

Beowulf

Beowulf Resources
http://www.georgetown.edu/irvinemj/english016/beowulf/beowulf.html
Bibliography, *Beowulf* in Old English and translated, information about Anglo-Saxon literature, images of the manuscript, and keyword search; part of the *Labyrinth* site at Georgetown University.

Electronic Beowulf, The
http://www.uky.edu/~kieman/BL/kportico.html
> Part of the Electronic Beowulf Project at the British Library (University of Kentucky), a huge database of digital images of the *Beowulf* manuscript, related manuscripts, and printed texts.

Berryman, John

RedFrog—Poems from the Planet Earth—John Berryman
http://redfrog.norconnect.no/~poems/poets/john_berryman.html
> Link to biography; search device for poetry (by word, phrase, or line); link to e-texts of a few poems.

Bishop, Elizabeth

EB Title Page
http://iberia.vassar.edu/bishop/
> Part of the personal page of Barbara Page, member of the Elizabeth Bishop Society; links to biography, bibliography, essays, the Elizabeth Bishop Society, and websites on related subjects; last revised October 31, 1997.

Blake, William

Blake Multimedia Project, The
http://www.fmdc.calpoly.edu/libarts/smarx/Blake/blakeproject.html
> "An approach to studying and teaching Blake using the tools of computer technology"; hypermedia archive of images and text as a course project at California Polytechnic University.

**William Blake Archive, The
http://jefferson.village.Virginia.EDU/blake/
> Hypermedia archive sponsored by the Library of Congress, the University of Virginia, and others, with full scholarly apparatus and beautiful, searchable images; links to search of text and image, e-texts, and selected bibliography; reviewed in *Choice*.

Boccaccio, Giovanni

Decameron Web, The
http://www.brown.edu/Research/Decameron/
> Page of links to bibliography, e-texts, maps, history, religion and literature, medieval society, and so forth.

Böll, Heinrich

Heinrich Böll Winner of the 1972 Nobel Prize in Literature
http://nobelprizes.com/nobel/literature/1972a.html
> Entry from the *Nobel Prize Internet Archive*.

Borges, Jorge Luis

Garden of Forking Paths: A Jorge Luis Borges Web Site, The
http://rpg.net/quail/libyrinth/borges/
    Links to biography, bibliography, criticism, quotations, online papers,
    films, tapes, bookstores, the Jorges Luis Borges Center, and other related
    sites; part of a personal page.

Boswell, James

ABC Scotland: James Boswell (1740–95)
http://www.geocities.com/Athens/Acropolis/9172/james_boswell.html
    Part of Scottish Writers on the Internet compiled by Andrew Crumey in
    1997; commercial site associated with *Amazon.com;* brief biographical
    note, links to books (to order or comment on).

Boswell's Life of Johnson, 1748
http://www.english.upenn.edu/~jlynch/Johnson/BLJ/blj48.html
    Edited from the two-volume Oxford edition of 1904 by Jack Lynch,
    fifth-year Ph.D. candidate in English literature at the University of Penn-
    sylvania; footnotes.

Brecht, Bertolt

Welcome to Bertolt Brecht Turns 100 Web Exhibition
http://www.usc.edu/isd/locations/collections/fml/Brecht/
    Online exhibition with many divisions pertaining to Brecht's life in exile
    in the United States; created by Marje Schuetze-Coburn, Feuchtwanger
    Librarian at the University of Southern California.

Bronte sisters

Anne Bronte (1820–1849)
http://www.mala.bc.ca/~mcneil/brontea.htm
    Malaspina Great Books links page.

Bronte Sisters, The
http://www2.sbbs.se/hp/cfalk/bronte1e.htm
    Part of Cecilia Falk's personal page (Swedish translator); links to books
    and information about the sisters, e-texts, biography, chronology, pictures,
    commentaries, and Haworth and the Irish Roots.

Charlotte Bronte (1816–1855)
http://www.mala.bc.ca/~mcneil/brontec.htm
    Malaspina Great Books links page.

Charlotte Bronte: An Overview

http://www.stg.brown.edu/projects/hypertext/landow/victorian/cbronte/
bronteov3.html
>   Part of the *Victorian Web;* pages include biography, works, literary and artistic relations, cultural, social and political contexts, religion and philosophy, science and technology, themes, and characterization.

Emily Bronte Page, The
http://homepages.enterprise.net/steph/emily.html
>   The usual: brief biography and many links; a Malaspina University College Great Books Five Star site.

Emily Jane Bronte (1818–1848)
http://www.mala.bc.ca/~mcneil/brontee.htm
>   *Malaspina Great Books* links page.

Brooks, Gwendolyn

Voices from the Gaps: Gwendolyn Brooks
http://www-engl.cla.umn.edu/lkd/vfg/Authors/GwendolynBrooks
>   A photograph, a poem, a biography, a bibliography, and two related links.

Browne, Thomas

Browne, Thomas
http://es.rice.edu/ES/humsoc/Galileo/Catalog/Files/browne.html
>   Compiled by Richard S. Westfall, Department of History and Philosophy of Science, Indiana University; schematic biography; list of sources.

Browning, Elizabeth Barrett

Elizabeth Barrett Browning: An Overview
http://www.stg.brown.edu/projects/hypertext/landow/victorian/ebb/
browning2ov.html
>   Part of the *Victorian Web;* pages of biography, other works, literary relations, cultural, social and political contexts, religion and philosophy, science and technology, themes, imagery, symbolism, and so forth.

Browning, Robert

Selected Poetry of Robert Browning (1812–1889)
http://library.utoronto.ca/www/utel/rp/authors/browning.html
>   Part of the University of Toronto English Department's selection of on-line poetry.

Büchner, Georg

Büchner, Georg: Woyzeck
http://endeavor.med.nyu.edu/lit-med/lit-med-db/webdocs/webdescrips/
buchner258-des-.html
> Brief consideration of Büchner in relation to medical issues; part of the
> *Literature, Arts and Medicine Database* site.

Bunyan, John

Encyclopedia.com—Results for Bunyan, John
http://www.encyclopedia.com/articles/02019.html
> Entry from *Electronic Library-Encyclopedia.com;* links to other sites
> (including pictures and e-texts); free sample of subscription service.

Life of John Bunyan and the Impact of His Allegory "The Pilgrim's Progress"
http://www.newlife.org/pilgrim.html
> Extended biographical and critical sketch with no author cited, offering
> more enthusiasm than scholarship; part of a site related to "Celestial
> City," a drama performed by the New Life Drama Company.

Burns, Robert

Robert Burns
http://www.dcs.gla.ac.uk/~jonathan/burns/
> Part of Jonathan Hogg's personal page (Hogg is a research student at the
> University of Glasgow); brief biography; three poems and other re-
> sources.

Burton, Robert

Robert Burton: Anatomy of Melancholy
http://humanitas.ucsb.edu/users/cstahmer/cogsci/burton.html
> Annotated bibliography of Burton's *The Anatomy of Melancholy;* page
> created by Carl Stahmer, a teacher in the University of California–Santa
> Barbara's English Department.

Byron, George Gordon, Lord

Byron: A Comprehensive Study of His Life and Work
http://www.geocities.com/athens/forum/9194/byron/bycover.html
> Fan page with many resources, including links to biography, chronology,
> letters, journals, portraits of Byron, and e-texts of his poetry.

Lord Byron Homepage, The
http://www.geocities.com/Athens/Acropolis/8916/byron.html

Fan page with links, including one to a site devoted to saving Newstead Abbey, Byron's home.

Selected Poetry of George Gordon, Lord Byron
http://library.utoronto.ca/www/utel/rp/authors/byron.html
University of Toronto's e-text collection.

Caedmon

Catholic Encyclopedia: St. Caedmon
http://www.knight.org/advent/cathen/03131c.htm
Entry from the *Catholic Encyclopedia*; page created by the New Advent.

Calderón de la Barca y Henao, Pedro

Calderón de la Barca y Henao, Pedro
http://encarta.msn.com/index/concise/0VOL11/01f90000.asp
Entry in *Encarta* online, an abridged version of the CD-ROM encyclopedia; links to related subjects and to additional web-searching resources.

Camus, Albert

Existentialism Albert Camus by Katharena Eiermann
http://members.aol.com/KatharenaE/private/Philo/Camus/camus.html
Camus home page with many links; conceived in the context of an existentialism site by Katharena Eiermann.

Carroll, Lewis

Lewis Carroll—Alice's Adventures in Wonderland
http://www.literature.org/Works/Lewis-Carroll/alice-in-wonderland/
Complete e-text version in the Online Literature Library.

Castle of Perseverance, The

Amazon.com: A Glance: Castle of Perseverance (Tudor Facsimile Texts, Old English Plays ; No. 1)
http://www.amazon.com/exec/obidos/ISBN%3D0404533019/
malaspgreatbooksA/002-1252488-1261664
Amazon.com advertisement for an edition of *The Castle of Perseverance* in a Tudor Facsimile Edition; links to related books in the electronic bookstore's stock.

Cather, Willa

Willa Cather (1873–1947)
http://www.mala.bc.ca/~mcneil/cather.htm
Malaspina Great Books links page.

Willa Cather Page
http://icg.fas.harvard.edu/~cather/
    Extremely brief biographical sketch followed by links to events, publica-
    tions, locations, quotations, biography, related sites, and home page of
    the Willa Cather Pioneer Memorial; fan page.

Céline, Louis-Ferdinand

Louis-Ferdinand Céline
http://www.levity.com/corduroy/celine.htm
    Biography and bibliography appearing in an online journal called
    Bohemian Ink.

Cervantes Saavedra, Miguel de

Don Quixote Exhibit, The
http://milton.mse.jhu.edu:8003/quixote/index.html
    Digital exhibit of translations and illustrations of Cervantes' famous
    novel; holdings of George Peabody Library, curated by professors at
    University of Johns Hopkins.

Miguel de Cervantes (1547–1616)
http://www.mala.bc.ca/~mcneil/cerv.htm
    Malaspina Great Books links page.

Chandler, Raymond

Raymond Chandler Online Library
http://www.byronpreiss.com/brooklyn/marlowe/chandler.htm
    Commercial site with biography followed by links to "detailed" biogra-
    phy, bibliography, and other mystery writers talking about Chandler.

Chaucer, Geoffrey

Baragona's Chaucer Home Page
http://www.vmi.edu/~english/chaucer.html
    Part of Alan Baragona's page (Baragona is a professor at the Virginia
    Military Institute); links to bibliographies, general bibliographies, hu-
    manities databases, and other sources related to Chaucer; designed pri-
    marily for a class.

Canterbury Tales Project, The
http://www.shef.ac.uk/uni/projects/ctp/index.html
    Page of links to information about Cambridge University's project to put
    all manuscripts of "The Canterbury Tales" on CD-ROM (includes links
    to other Chaucer-related sites).

Geoffrey Chaucer (ca. 1340–1400)
http://www.mala.bc.ca/~mcneil/chaucer.htm
>*Malaspina Great Books* links page.

Great Books Index—Chaucer
http://books.mirror.org/gb.chaucer.html
>Index to Chaucer's writings; links to online editions, more information about Chaucer, and other pages within the *Great Books Index.*

Chekhov, Anton

Anton Chekhov (1860–1904)
http://www.mala.bc.ca/~mcneil/chekhov.htm
>*Malaspina Great Books* links page.

Churchill, Caryl

Caryl Churchill—Introduction
http://www.el.net/~alexis/thesis/intro.html
>Essay entitled "Who Is Caryl Churchill and What Does It Mean to be a Feminist Playwright?"; part of Alexis Lloyd's personal page (Lloyd is a student at Vassar College); written in 1996 for a B.A. program in drama.

El Cid

Lay of the Cid, The
http://sunsite.berkeley.edu/OMACL/Cid/
>Part of the Berkeley Digital Library SunSite; background, bibliography, and links to e-text.

Coleridge, Samuel Taylor

Lake Poets, The
http://www.globalnet.co.uk/~burge01/page52.htm
>British fan site devoted to links for Wordsworth and Coleridge.

Samuel Taylor Coleridge (1772–1834)
http://www.mala.bc.ca/~mcneil/cole.htm   .
>*Malaspina Great Books* links page.

Samuel Taylor Coleridge—Biography
http://www.english.upenn.edu/~jlynch/Frank/Coleridg/bio.html
>Biographical essay with many links to Coleridge's connections.

S. T. Coleridge Home Page
http://www.lib.virginia.edu/etext/stc/Coleridge/stc.html
>Page of links for Coleridge, including poetry, literary theory and criti-

cism, political commentary and journalism, science, philosophy, theology, and letters.

Collins, Wilkie

Wilkie Collins Appreciation Page
http://www.ozemail.com.au/~drgrigg/wilkie.html
Enthusiastic fan's links page for Collins.

Conrad, Joseph

Candice Bradley's Heart of Darkness Lecture
http://www.lawrence.edu/~bradleyc/heart.html
"Africa and Africans in Conrad's Heart of Darkness," a Lawrence University Freshman Studies Lecture by Candice Bradley, associate professor of anthropology.

Cowley, Abraham

Daniel Kinney: The Abraham Cowley Text and Image Archive: University of Virginia
http://etext.virginia.edu/kinney/
Part of the University of Virginia Library's invaluable e-text collection, directed by Daniel Kinney, Department of English.

Cowper, William

Selected Poetry of William Cowper (1731–1800)
http://www.library.utoronto.ca/www/utel/rp/authors/cowper.html
Page provided by members of the Department of English, University of Toronto; links to poetry; index by poet, first line, date, and keyword; criticism and links to related materials.

Crabbe, George

George Crabbe (1754–1832) The Village: Book I
http://library.utoronto.ca/www/utel/rp/poems/crabbe1b.html
Page provided by members of the Department of English, University of Toronto; reprints *The Village*: Book I; links to other poems by Crabbe, the poet's life and works.

Crane, Hart

Brad Lucas' Hart Crane Home Page
http://unr.edu/homepage/brad/hart/crane.html
Part of (fan, academic) Brad Lucas's personal page; links to reference

and research sources; people, vendors, and miscellaneous; essays, papers, and explications; bibliography.

Crane, Stephen

Resources for the Study of Stephen Crane
http://www.d.umn.edu/~sadams/Crane.htm
  Biography, bibliography, and four links.

Stephen Crane: Man, Myth, and Legend
http://www.cwrl.utexas.edu/~mmaynard/Crane/crane.html
  Part of Michelle Maynard's course "Masterworks of American Literature" at the University of Texas.; links to biography, original sound clips of three of Crane's works; papers, research projects, themes, issues, and so on.

Crashaw, Richard

Richard Crashaw (1613–1649)
http://www.luminarium.org/sevenlit/crashaw/
  Part of *Luminarium*'s *Early 17th Century* site.

Cruz, Sor Juana Inés de la

Sor Juana Inés de La Cruz (1648–1695)
http://www.writepage.com/others/sorjuana.htm
  Malaspina Great Books links page.

Sor Juana Inés de la Cruz Project, The
http://www.dartmouth.edu/~sorjuana/
  Sponsored by the Department of Spanish and Portuguese at Dartmouth College; an attractive site with images and many scholarly links.

cummings, e.e.

e.e. cummings
http://www.imsa.edu/~junkee/cummings.html
  Part of the *Mining Co.* website; biography and some links, but all poems have recently been removed from the site by action of the E.E. Cummings Copyright Trust.

Dante Alighieri

Dante
http://www.providence.edu/dwc/medante.htm
  Page of annotated links for Dante, various and interesting.

Dante Alighieri (1265–1321)
http://www.mala.bc.ca/~mcneil/dante.htm
   Malaspina Great Books links page.

**ILTweb Digital Dante*
http://www.ilt.columbia.edu/projects/dante/index.html
   Elaborate site presented by the Department of Italian at Columbia University; links to Image Collections and to translations of the *Comedy* (Longfellow and Mandelbaum, both separately and in line-by-line comparison); many other links and resources.

Renaissance Dante in Print (1472–1629)
http://www.nd.edu/~italnet/Dante/
   Exhibition presenting Renaissance editions of Dante's *Divine Comedy* from the Dante Collection at the University of Notre Dame and from the Newberry Library.

Defoe, Daniel

Daniel Defoe (1660–1731)
http://www.mala.bc.ca/~mcneil/defoe.htm
   Malaspina Great Books links page.

Project Gutenberg—Catalog by Author—Defoe, Daniel, 1661?–1731
http://www.gutenberg.net/_authors/defoe_daniel_.html
   Extensive list of Defoe e-texts from Project Gutenberg.

DeLillo, Don

Don DeLillo's America
http://haas.berkeley.edu/~gardner/delillo.html
   Part of Curt Gardner's personal page; links to biography, bibliography, novels, stories, plays, interviews, profiles, quotations, criticism, reviews, information on DeLillo's books, and discussion group.

Desai, Anita

Anita Desai: An Overview
http://www.stg.brown.edu/projects/hypertext/landow/post/desai/desaiov.html
   Part of the *Postcolonial and Postimperial Web* created by George P. Landow, professor of English and art history, Brown University; links to biography, postcolonial literature, literary relations, history, and so on.

Dickens, Charles

Charles Dickens (1812–1870)
http://www.mala.bc.ca/~mcneil/dickens.htm
   Malaspina Great Books links page.

Dickens Page, The
http://lang.nagoya-u.ac.jp/~matsuoka/Dickens.html
> Part of Mitsuharu Matsuoka's personal page (professor at Nagoya University, Japan); links to e-texts, biography, filmography, Dickens Fellowship, Dickens Society, home pages, chronology, bibliography, and so on.

Dickens Project, The
http://humwww.ucsc.edu/dickens/index.html
> Scholarly consortium at the California State University–Stanislans; links to institutional business and Dickens sites.

Dickinson, Emily

***Dickinson Electronic Archives*
http://jefferson.village.virginia.edu/dickinson/
> Some images of handwritten letters, full collection of letters to Susan Dickinson, student work, and more in an innovative approach to Dickinson; limited access to some portions; supported by the Institute of Advanced Technology in the Humanities at the University of Virginia, Charlottesville; created by Martha Nell Smith, 1997.

Emily Dickinson (1830–1886)
http://www.csustan.edu/english/reuben/pal/chap4/dickinson.html#themes
> Part of a personal page created by Paul P. Reuben (Department of English, California State University); themes in Dickinson's poetry and study questions for class.

Emily Dickinson Page
http://www.planet.net/pkrisxle/emily/dickinson.html
> Links to 460 of Dickinson's poems online, poems about her, biography, e-mail discussion list, a list of frequently asked questions, a page of Dickinsonian products and services; created by Paul E. Black (computer scientist).

Dinesen, Isaak

Karen Blixen Museum, The
http://www.dis.dk/kultur/karenb/kbtekst.e.html
> Museum in Copenhagen devoted to Isaak Dinesen; links to biography, images of her paintings, and others (mostly museum business).

Donne, John

John Donne (1572–1631)
http://www.luminarium.org/sevenlit/donne/
> Anniina Jokinen's page on *Luminarium* site; links to quotes, biography, works (e-texts), essays, books, and so on.

Dostoevsky, Feodor

Fyodor Dostoevsky (1821–1881)
http://www.mala.bc.ca/~mcneil/dost.htm
   Malaspina Great Books links page.

Fyodor Dostoevsky: The Website
http://stange.simplenet.com/dostoevsky/
   Links to Dostoevsky in the words of others, bibliography of published
   works, a chronology of events, critical essays, study guides, e-texts, other
   Dostoevsky sites, and other related sites; part of a personal page.

Douglass, Frederick

Frederick Douglass
http://www.history.rochester.edu/class/douglass/HOME.html
   Biography of Douglass by Sandra Thomas; links to the slave years, the
   beginnings of an abolitionist, the Rochester years, the Civil War years,
   life after the Thirteenth Amendment, chronology, and further reading.

Dream of the Rood, The

Dream of the Rood, The
http://www.mta.ca/faculty/humanities/religious/3041/dreamrd.htm
   Provided by the Department of Religious Studies at Mount Allison University; links to e-text of the poem; analysis, history, and description of
   the Ruthwell Cross monument.

Dryden, John

John Dryden
http://ernie.bgsu.edu/~smorgan/publick/dryden.html
   Part of the *Restoration Drama Web Site;* biographical information; links
   to other authors.

Selected Poetry and Prose of John Dryden (1631–1700)
http://library.utoronto.ca/www/utel/rp/authors/dryden.html
   Prepared by members of the Department of English at the University of
   Toronto; index to poems and prose.

Dunbar, Paul Laurence

Paul Laurence Dunbar Homepage
http://www.udayton.edu/~dunbar/
   Site maintained by the Black Alumni Chronicle of the University of
   Dayton; links to biography, pictures, other web sources, poems, and in-

formation about Herbert Woodward Martin, who performs Dunbar's poetry.

Eliot, George

George Eliot: An Overview
http://www.stg.brown.edu/projects/hypertext/landow/victorian/eliot/
eliotov.html
> Part of the *Victorian Web;* links to biography, works (e-texts), literary re-
> lations, themes, symbolism, genre, visual arts, characterization, narra-
> tion, religion, philosophy, and so on.

Eliot, T. S.

City Honors T. S. Eliot Page
http://cityhonors.buffalo.k12.ny.us/city/reference/English/auth/eli.html
> Enormous links page for Eliot; both this site and the following one are
> called "The T.S. Eliot Page," but they are very different.

T. S. Eliot Page, The
http://virtual.park.uga.edu/~232/eliot.taken.html
> Part of fan Bruce Ong's personal page; links to *AltaVista* search results,
> biography, e-texts, a recording of Eliot reading his own poetry, and other
> links not available anymore (including Ong's home page).

T. S. (Thomas Stearns) Eliot (1888–1965)
http://www.mala.bc.ca/~mcneil/eliotts.htm
> *Malaspina Great Books* links page.

Ellison, Ralph

San Antonio College LitWeb Ralph Ellison Page
http://www.accd.edu/sac/english/bailey/ellisonr.htm
> Ellison bibliography, some items of which are linked; part of an Ameri-
> can literature index compiled by Roger Blackwell Bailey.

Emerson, Ralph Waldo

Ralph Waldo Emerson (1803–1882)
http://www.mala.bc.ca/~mcneil/emerson.htm
> *Malaspina Great Books* links page.

Ralph Waldo Emerson—American Author, Poet and Philosopher
http://www2.lucidcafe.com/lucidcafe/lucidcafe/library/96may/emerson.html
> Part of *Lucidcafe* site; biographical note, poem "What is Success?"; links
> to Emerson resources, other authors and poets in the Lucidcafe Library,
> other sites about Emerson, books about him, and works by him.

Euripides

Euripides (ca. 485–406 B.C.)
http://www.mala.bc.ca/~mcneil/euri.htm
   Malaspina Great Books links page.

Euripides
http://www-adm.pdx.edu/user/sinq/greekciv/arts/greeklit/euripide.htm
   Biographical page within Greek literature site created by Angela De-
   Haven, sophomore at Portland State University; links within site.

Everyman

Everyman (ca. 1475?)
http://www.mala.bc.ca/~mcneil/every.htm
   Malaspina Great Books links page.

Everyman
http://etext.lib.virginia.edu/etcbin/browse-mixed-new?id=AnoEver&tag=
public&images=images/modeng&data=/lv1/Archive/mideng-parsed
   E-text of *Everyman* from the Electronic Text Center at the University of
   Virginia; information about the text (printed and online edition); links to
   other e-texts.

Faulkner, William

**William Faulkner on the Web*
http://www.mcsr.olemiss.edu/~egjbp/faulkner/faulkner.html
   Truly remarkable page of links; imaginative, thorough, and very extensive; from Ole Miss's Department of English.

Fielding, Henry

San Antonio College LitWeb Henry Fielding Page
http://www.accd.edu/sac/english/bailey/fielding.htm
   Biographical sketch; part of *SAC Restoration and Eighteenth Century
   Literature Index*.

Fitzgerald, F. Scott

***F. Scott Fitzgerald Centenary Home Page*
http://www.sc.edu/fitzgerald/index.html
   Remarkable site devoted to Fitzgerald, with bibliographies, a chronology, e-texts, photographs, essays, articles, and even recordings of Fitzgerald reading; sponsored by the University of South Carolina; reviewed
   in *Choice*.

Flaubert, Gustave

Flaubert, Gustave
http://encarta.msn.com/index/concise/0vol05/00869000.asp
> Entry in *Encarta* online, an abridged version of the CD-ROM encyclope-
> dia; links to related subjects and to additional web-searching resources.

France, Marie de

Lais of Marie de France Study Guide, The
http://www.wsu.edu:8080/~brians/love-in-the-arts/marie.html
> Part of Paul Brian's personal page with study guides designed for his lit-
> erature students; this one is based on the Penguin text.

Freeman, Mary Wilkins

Mary E. Wilkins Freeman
http://www.gonzaga.edu/faculty/campbell/enl311/freeman.htm
> Freeman page with links to bibliographies, e-texts of her work, and pho-
> tographic images.

Freneau, Philip

Philip Freneau (1752–1832)
http://www.csustan.edu/english/reuben/pal/chap2/freneau.html
> Part of "Perspectives in American Literature: A Research and Reference
> Guide" by Paul B. Reuben; Freneau bibliography, some analysis, and
> study questions.

Frost, Robert

Bedford Books: Literature Links, Frost
http://www.bedfordbooks.com/litlinks/frost.html
> Links five sites devoted to Robert Frost; each site is described and evalu-
> ated; part of the Bedford Books presentation of their published authors.

Fry, Christopher

Fry, Christopher
http://encarta.msn.com/index/concise/0vol1E/039b7000.asp
> Part of *Encarta* online, an abridged version of CD-ROM encyclopedia;
> links to related subjects and to additional web-searching resources.

Fugard, Athol

Fugard, Athol: The Road to Mecca

http://endeavor.med.nyu.edu/lit-med/lit-med-db/webdocs/webdescrips/
fugard842-des-.html
> Part of *Medical Humanities* site; brief discussion of Fugard's play in relation to such categories as aging, loneliness, and rebellion.

García Lorca, Federico

Federico Garcia Lorca
http://www.powerup.com.au/~liesl/lorca.htm
> Fan site with links to translated poems; the author admits he has no rights to the works he is displaying and asks not to be sued.

García Márquez, Gabriel

**Macondo: A Gabriel García Márquez Web Site*
http://rpg.net/quail/libyrinth/gabo/
> Large, rather beautiful site, exploring many aspects of García Márquez's life and work; imaginative presentation.

Genesis

Reading Genesis: Introduction
http://www.emory.edu/UDR/BLUMENTHAL/GenIntro.html
> Sophisticated commentary by David Blumenthal, professor of Judaic studies at Emory.

Gilman, Charlotte Perkins

Charlotte Perkins Gilman, The Yellow Wallpaper (1899)
http://www.library.csi.cuny.edu/dept/history/lavender/ywdiscuss.html
> Brief biography, study questions, and further resources for studying Gilman; prepared by Catherine Lavender, Department of History, College of Staten Island, City University of New York.

Yellow Wallpaper Site, The
http://www.cwrl.utexas.edu/~daniel/amlit/wallpaper/wallpaper.html
> Site constructed by Daniel Anderson's students for a course in American literature at Smith College; includes discussion group and electronic newsletter on Gilman.

Goethe, Johann Wolfgang von

Johann Wolfgang von Goethe (1749–1832)
http://www.mala.bc.ca/~mcneil/goethe.htm
> *Malaspina Great Books* links page.

Johann Wolfgang von Goethe by Katharena Eiermann

http://members.aol.com/KatharenaE/private/Pweek/Goethe/goethe.html
> *Great Books* site prepared by Katharena Eiermann with a large range of
> linked resources: screen after screen of Goethe information.

Goldsmith, Oliver

CELT: Oliver Goldsmith
http://www.ucc.ie/celt/goldsmith.html
> Part of the online project of Irish literary texts; link to e-text of "The De-
> serted Village."

Gordimer, Nadine

Nadine Gordimer: An Overview
http://www.stg.brown.edu/projects/hypertext/landow/post/gordimer/
gordimerov.html
> Links in sixteen categories relating to Gordimer's work, including post-
> colonial overview, literary relations, and narrative structure; created by
> George P. Landow, who designed the *Victorian Web.*

Grass, Günther

*TPCN—Great Quotations (Quotes) by Günther Grass to Inspire
and Motivate You to Achieve Your Dreams!*
http://www.cyber-nation.com/victory/quotations/authors/quotes_grass_
gunther.html
> Bizarre (and very commercial) site with "Quotes to Inspire You" from a
> number of noted authors, including Grass; recommended only for those
> who enjoy exotic couplings of art and business.

Gray, Thomas

Selected Poetry of Thomas Gray (1716–1771)
http://library.utoronto.ca/www/utel/rp/authors/gray.html
> E-texts of Gray's poetry from the collection of the English Department
> of the University of Toronto.

Hansberry, Lorraine

San Antonio College LitWeb Lorraine Hansberry Page, The
http://www.accd.edu/sac/english/bailey/hansberr.htm
> Photograph of the author; bibliography of her works; brief list of links;
> part of an *American Women Writers* site.

Hardy, Thomas

Hardy in Dorset
http://www.prestigeweb.com/hardy/hardy.html
Site of the Thomas Hardy On-line Society; associated with *Amazon.com*.

Thomas Hardy Resource Library
http://pages.ripco.com:8080/~mws/hardy.html
Fan site with links to e-text, biography, media, Dorset, and other Hardy links pages.

Hawthorne, Nathaniel

**Nathaniel Hawthorne
http://eldred.ne.mediaone.net/nh/hawthorne.html
Author home page of unusual range and size; links to hundreds of sources related to Hawthorne; rather breezily presented, but invaluable.

Nathaniel Hawthorne (1804–1864)
http://www.mala.bc.ca/~mcneil/haw.htm
Malaspina Great Books links page.

Hemingway, Ernest

Ernest Hemingway (1899–1961)
http://www.mala.bc.ca/~mcneil/hemingway.htm
Malaspina Great Books links page.

Ultimate Hemingway Site, The
http://members.aol.com/mwilson311/Hemingway/Papabib.htm
Oversold by its title, this site is an annotated bibliography of works about Hemingway with no links.

Herbert, George

George Herbert
http://members.aol.com/ericblomqu/herbert.htm
E-texts of a number of Herbert poems; on an America Online fan site; part of *Sonnet Central*.

George Herbert (1593–1633)
http://www.luminarium.org/sevenlit/herbert/index.html
Part of the *Luminarium* site.

Herrick, Robert

Robert Herrick (1591–1674)
http://www.luminarium.org/sevenlit/herrick/index.html
Part of the *Luminarium* site.

Homer

Homer (ca. 900 B.C.)
http://www.mala.bc.ca/~mcneil/homer.htm
   Malaspina Great Books links page.

Homer's Iliad and Odyssey
http://hyperion.advanced.org/19300/data/homer.htm
   Home page for Homer; links to the *Iliad,* the *Odyssey,* e-texts, Homer's
   Greece, Homer's history, comparative mythology, mailing lists, references, and so on; developed by students for *Thinkquest.*

Hopkins, Gerard Manley

Gerard Manley Hopkins Overview
http://www.stg.brown.edu/projects/hypertext/landow/victorian/hopkins/
gmhov.html
   Part of the *Victorian Web,* with links to a broad spectrum of categories,
   ranging from politics to literary relations.

Housman, A. E.

Housman, A. E. 1896. A Shropshire Lad.
http://www.cc.columbia.edu/acis/bartleby/housman/index.html
   E-text in the Bartleby Archive; links to individual poems.

Howard, Henry, Earl of Surrey

Henry Howard, Earl of Surrey (1517–1547)
http://www.luminarium.org/renlit/henry.htm
   Part of the *Luminarium* site.

Howells, William Dean

William Dean Howells Society Home Page
http://www.gonzaga.edu/faculty/campbell/howells/index.html
   Many standard literary links, plus some unusual ones: to a Howells
   discussion list and various conferences and associations that focus on
   him.

Hughes, Langston

Book Shelf: Langston Hughes
http://www.blackstripe.com/books/hughes.html
   Partially annotated list of Hughes's works, provided by Black Stripe, a
   gay and lesbian Black bookstore.

Hurston, Zora Neale

Zora Neale Hurston, American Author
http://www-hsc.usc.edu/~gallaher/hurston/hurston.html
> Fan page with a lot of expressed enthusiasm, a bit of biography, and some links.

Ibsen, Henrik

**Ibsen Links*
http://www.ibsen.net/ibsenlinker_en.htm
> Surprisingly diverse links for Ibsen with a great many connections to Norwegian institutions and places that honor him.

Jacobs, Harriet Ann

Harriet Ann Jacobs (1813–1897)
http://www.georgetown.edu/bassr/heath/syllabuild/iguide/jacobs.html
> Study guide site designed to aid in teaching Jacobs's work; excellent aid in planning a syllabus.

James, Henry

***Henry James Scholar's Guide to Web Sites, The*
http://www.newpaltz.edu/~hathaway/
> Huge links site with (it seems) every conceivable connection to James listed; written by Robert D. Hathaway, professor of English, State University of New York–New Paltz.

Jewett, Sarah Orne

Jewett, Sarah Orne. 1910. The Country of the Pointed Firs.
http://www.cc.columbia.edu/acis/bartleby/jewett/
> E-text; part of the Bartleby Archive.

Johnson, Samuel

Johnson Society of London—A Samuel Johnson bibliography
http://www.nbbl.demon.co.uk/JSL7.html
> Mostly bibliography, with some attention to the business and pleasure of the Samuel Johnson Society.

Samuel Johnson Sound Bite Page, The
http://www.samueljohnson.com/
> Not very serious, perhaps, but Frank Lynch's quotes from Johnson make an entertaining and unusual literary website.

Jonson, Ben

**Ben Jonson (1572–1637)*
http://www.luminarium.org/sevenlit/jonson/
> Part of the invaluable *Luminarium* site, with links, images, and, given the right plug-ins, music to enhance the study of Jonson and his age.

Joyce, James

**Work in Progress: A James Joyce Website*
http://www.2street.com/joyce/
> Imaginatively created and maintained by R. L. Callahan of Temple University; links to online site resources, biographical timeline, Joyce discussion groups, maps of Dublin, digitized audio recordings of Joyce reading his work, and much more.

Julian of Norwich

Bibliography for the British Medieval Mystics
http://www.mindspring.com/~mccolman/bibliography.htm
> Julian of Norwich bibliography in the series on British Medieval Mystics; no links in the bibliography, but site has one connection to a biographical sketch.

Kafka, Franz

Castle Home Page, The
http://family.knick.net/thecastle/
> Quite elaborate, rather confusing fan page with lots of Kafka resources and such extras as a link to "creative writing I have done on Kafka"; determining who the author of the site happens to be is not easy.

Constructing Franz Kafka
http://info.pitt.edu/~kafka/intro.html
> Large and varied list of links for Kafka, predominantly in English.

Franz Kafka (1883–1924)
http://www.mala.bc.ca/~mcneil/kafka.htm
> *Malaspina Great Books* links page.

Keats, John

Keats-Shelley Journal Home Page
http://www.luc.edu/publications/keats-shelley/ksjweb.htm
> Much information about the journal itself, but also links to very helpful bibliographies and web resources, both general and author-specific.

Kempe, Margery

Margery Kempe (ca. 1373–1438)
http://www.luminarium.org/medlit/kempe.htm
   Part of the *Luminarium* site.

Laforgue, Jules

Laforgue, Jules
http://encarta.msn.com/index/concise/0vol34/06427000.asp
   Entry in *Encarta* online, an abridged version of the CD-ROM encyclopedia; links to related subjects and to additional web-searching resources.

Lawrence, D. H.

D. H. Lawrence Index Page
http://home.clara.net/rananim/lawrence/
   Gateway to a very elaborate Lawrence fan site, with dozens of links; content suggested by the Rananim Society, an e-mail discussion group devoted to Lawrence.

Lazarillo de Tormes

Lazarillo Project
http://www.oit.itd.umich.edu/WIP/ForeignLanguages/LazarilloProject.html
   Description of a project to create an interactive program related to
   Lazarillo de Tormes; announced by the Office of Instructional Technology at the University of Michigan.

LeGuin, Ursula K.

Ursula K. LeGuin—Related Works
http://www.non.com/books/LeGuin_Ursula_s.html
   Amazon.com's (quite large) list of books about LeGuin and her works;
   links to purchasing process.

L'Engle, Madeleine

Madeleine L'Engle Fan Homepage, The
http://wwwvms.utexas.edu/~eithlan/lengle.html
   Fan site with a little bibliography, a little biography, a few links, and a lot
   of unofficial enthusiasm.

Lewis, C. S.

C. S. Lewis Foundation—Living the Legacy!
http://www.cslewis.org/

Foundation advertisement with links to a timeline of Lewis's life and other connections of a much more businesslike sort.

C. S. Lewis and the Inklings Home Page
http://ernie.bgsu.edu/~edwards/lewis.html
Site devoted to Lewis and his fellow Inklings with many links to literary and organizational sites; maintained by Bruce L. Edwards, professor of English at Bowling Green State University.

London, Jack

***Jack London Collection, The*
http://sunsite.berkeley.edu/London/
Part of the *Berkeley Digital Library Sunsite;* an impressive collection of novels, stories, letters, telegrams, and photographs in the Bancroft Library.

Lope de Vega Carpio, Félix

Vega, Lope de—Encarta® Concise Encyclopedia Article
http://encarta.msn.com/index/conciseindex/21/02115000.htm
Entry in *Encarta* online.

Lowell, Robert

Robert Lowell Papers
http://www.lib.utexas.edu/Libs/HRC/fa/lowell.hp.html
Information detailing contents of the Robert Lowell papers in the Harry Hansom Humanities Research Centre at the University of Texas.; links to biography and indexes of Lowell's work.

Machado de Assis, Joaquim

Joaquim Maria Machado de Assis
http://www.interlog.com/~artbiz/machado.html
Colorful, simple home page for Machado de Assis, by a Brazilian journalism student.

Mallarmé, Stéphane

Mallarmé, Stéphane
http://encarta.msn.com/index/concise/0VOL0C/016e5000.asp
Entry in *Encarta* online, an abridged version of the CD-ROM encyclopedia; links to related subjects and to additional web-searching resources.

Malory, Sir Thomas

When Malory Met Arthur

http://jackfritscher.com/fr02005.html
> Site constructed from Jack Fritscher's M.A. thesis, with a consolidated list of various Arthurian links.

Mann, Thomas

Thomas Mann Winner of the 1929 Nobel Prize in Literature
http://www.almaz.com/nobel/literature/1929a.html
> Entry from the *Nobel Prize Internet Archive.*

Mansfield, Katherine

Katherine Mansfield (1888–1923)
http://www.mala.bc.ca/~MCNEIL/mans.htm
> *Malaspina Great Books* links page.

Marlowe, Christopher

Christopher Marlowe (1564–1593)
http://www.luminarium.org/renlit/marlowe.htm
> Part of the *Luminarium* site.

Marvell, Andrew

Andrew Marvell (1621–1678)
http://www.luminarium.org/sevenlit/marvell/index.html
> Part of the *Luminarium* site.

McCullers, Carson

EducETH-McCullers,Carson
http://educeth.ethz.ch/english/readinglist/mccullers,carson.html
> Part of an education-oriented site for students and teachers; plenty of information about McCullers, despite emphasis on exchange of views.

Melville, Herman

***The Life and Works of Herman Melville*
http://www.melville.org/
> Joint scholarly effort to provide the best of Melville on the Internet; an enormous, impressive list of links.

Meredith, George

George Meredith Overview
http://www.stg.brown.edu/projects/hypertext/landow/victorian/meredith/meredithov.html
> Part of the *Victorian Web.*

Miller, Arthur

Concordance to Miller, Death of a Salesman
http://www.konbib.nl/dutchess.ned/18/06/info-0289.html
> Just what the title says: a concordance to *The Death of a Salesman*, compiled by the Dutch Electronic Subject Service. Why?

Milton, John

John Milton: The Milton-L Home Page
http://www.urich.edu/~creamer/milton/
> Site of a discussion group devoted to Milton, with links to chronology, e-texts, images, audio, articles, book reviews, events, *Milton Review*, Milton Transcription Project, and other resources.

Mishima Yukio

FringeWare Inc.—Bio: Yukio Mishima
http://www.fringeware.com/subcult/Yukio_Mishima.html
> Gay-oriented site with a lot of biographical information on Mishima in a rather strange format (white print on black); many esoteric links.

Mistral, Gabriela

Gabriela Mistral Winner of the 1945 Nobel Prize in Literature
http://nobelprizes.com/nobel/literature/1945a.html
> Biographical sketch and links on the *Nobel Prize Internet Archive*.

Molière, Jean Baptiste Poquelin

Molière
http://encarta.msn.com/index/concise/0vol09/00fa2000.asp
> Entry in *Encarta* online, an abridged version of the CD-ROM encyclopedia; links to related subjects and to additional web-searching resources.

Montaigne, Michel de

Michel de Montaigne
http://www.orst.edu/instruct/phl302/philosophers/montaigne.html
> Biography and timeline for Montaigne.

Moore, Marianne

Marianne Moore
http://www.cwrl.utexas.edu/~slatin/20c_poetry/projects/lives/mm.html
> Fan site with links to a few poems and some additional resources.

More, Thomas

St. Thomas More Web Page
http://pw2.netcom.com/~rjs474/thomasmore.html
> Links-only page; commercial site with connections to the Thomas More Bookstore and Thomas More Society, plus some academic and tourist sites.

Morrison, Toni

Anniina's Toni Morrison Page
http://www.luminarium.org/contemporary/tonimorrison/toni.htm
> One of the sites on African-American women writers produced by Aniina Jokinen, whose web pages are remarkably attractive and useful; links to biographies, bibliographies, interview, and other sites.

Navarre, Marguerite de

Heptameron Study Guide
http://www.auburn.edu/~mitrege/eh220web/study-guides/heptameron.html
> Study guide by George Mitrevski of the Department of Foreign Languages at Auburn University.

Neruda, Pablo

Links to Pablo Neruda
http://escuela.med.puc.cl/Departamentos/Pediatria/Pediat.2002.html
> Links-only pages; fan site.

O'Connor, Flannery

Links to Other Flannery O'Connor Related Sites
http://peacock.gac.peachnet.edu/~sc/links.html
> Links page sponsored by Flannery O'Connor Collection of the Ina Dillard Russell Library at Georgia College and State University, Milledgeville; ample coverage of the range of O'Connor sites.

O'Neill, Eugene

Eugene Gladstone O'Neill Winner of the 1936 Nobel Prize in Literature
http://nobelprizes.com/nobel/literature/1936a.html
> Mostly a links page: several for O'Neill specifically; several to the *Nobel Prize Internet Archive.*

Owen, Wilfred

***The Wilfred Owen Multimedia Digital Archive*
http://firth.nat.corp.ox.ac.uk/jtap/

Images of manuscripts, video clips from World War I and recent film representations of the war; option to create, annotate, and save one's own path through the archive.

Paine, Thomas

Thomas Paine National Historical Assoc.
http://www.mediapro.net/cdadesign/paine/
Malaspina Great Books Five Star site with a large archive of e-texts of Paine's works.

Paz, Octavio

Octavio Paz Winner of the 1990 Nobel Prize in Literature
http://nobelprizes.com/nobel/literature/1990a.html
Links to specific Paz sites and to the *Nobel Prize Internet Archive.*

Pérez Galdós, Benito

Pérez Galdós Editions Project, The
http://www.shef.ac.uk/uni/projects/gep/
Links for the study of Pérez Galdós and to introduce the Editions Project.

Pirandello, Luigi

Companion to Pirandello Studies, A
http://info.greenwood.com/books/0313257/0313257140.html
Description and chapter titles from a new book on Pirandello being published by Greenwood Press.

Luigi Pirandello Winner of the 1934 Nobel Prize in Literature
http://www.almaz.com/nobel/literature/1934a.html
Very brief, simple author page on the *Nobel Prize Internet Archive.*

Plato

Plato (428 BC–347 BC)
http://www.mala.bc.ca/~mcneil/plato.htm
Malaspina Great Books links page.

Socratic Dialectic, The: An On-Line, Interactive Version of Plato's Gorgias
http://www.dfw.net/~sherrin/plato.html
Student project for a humanities course; users may adopt Athenian personae and interact with Socrates as presented in the Gorgias.

Poe, Edgar Allan

Poe Decoder, The
http://www.poedecoder.com/

Site maintained by a (sort of) Poe fan club intent on presenting its own criticism and interpretations; some links to other Poe resources.

Pope, Alexander

Alexander Pope Page
http://www.shepherd.wvnet.edu/~maustin/authors/pope.html
Part of a syllabus for an eighteenth-century literature class; links to other Pope resource pages and e-texts.

Porter, Katharine Anne

Katharine Anne Porter (1890–1980)
http://www.georgetown.edu/bassr/heath/syllabuild/iguide/porter.html
Guide to syllabi production, focusing on techniques and materials for presenting Porter in the classroom.

Pound, Ezra

***Ezra Pound on the Web*
http://www.english.udel.edu/mkraus/pound.html
Links page maintained by Manuel Kraus at the University of Delaware with connections to general sources on Pound, scholarly journal on Pound and modernism, a listserv, hypertext projects, Pound's poetry on line, and online scholarship concerning him.

Proust, Marcel

Marcel Proust (1871–1922)
http://www.mala.bc.ca/~mcneil/proust.htm
Malaspina Great Books links page.

Racine, Jean Baptiste

Racine, Jean Baptiste
http://encarta.msn.com/index/concise/0vol24/0453a000.asp
Entry in *Encarta* online, an abridged version of the CD-ROM encyclopedia; links to related subjects and to additional web-searching resources.

Radcliffe, Ann

Ann Radcliffe: Poems
http://www.english.upenn.edu/~mgamer/Romantic/radcliffepoems.html
E-texts of Radcliffe's poems edited by Michael Gamer of the English Department at the University of Pennsylvania.

Reed, Ishmael

Ishmael Reed by Spring
http://www.math.buffalo.edu/~sww/reed/reed_ishmael0.html
> Fan page for Reed with links to biography, bibliography, "Reed Speaks," and others; disclaimer stating that the pages (created by Big Mouff) are not affiliated with Reed in any way.

Richardson, Samuel

Valencia West LRC—Richardson, Samuel
http://valencia.cc.fl.us/lrcwest/richardson.html
> Unlinked bibliography for Richardson; part of *Author Pathfinders* site maintained by Valencia Community College West Campus.

Rilke, Rainer Maria

Beauty and Love in Letters
http://www.cc.gatech.edu/grads/b/Gary.N.Boone/love_in_letters.html
> Excerpt from Rilke's "Letters to a Young Poet" presented as part of a site entitled the *Beauty and Love Page*.

Rimbaud, Jean Nicholas-Arthur

Jean Nicholas-Arthur Rimbaud
http://www.emination.co.uk/features/sean/sean.htm
> Extremely brief biographical sketch with a link to "filth, depravity, drink, drugs"; presented by something called Sleaze Nation Ltd. in the United Kingdom.

Robinson, Edwin Arlington

Edwin Arlington Robinson IHAS: Poet
http://www.pbs.org/wnet/ihas/poet/robinson.html
> Brief biography and texts of three poems that were set to music by composer John Duke; featured in *I Hear America Singing,* a PBS special.

Roethke, Theodore

Theodore Roethke IHAS: Poet
http://www.pbs.org/wnet/ihas/poet/roethke.html
> Brief biography and text of "The Snake," a poem that became one of the concert songs featured in *I Hear America Singing,* a PBS special.

Rojas, Fernando de

La Celestina
http://web.isbe.state.il.us/msmith/celestina/index.htm
> E-text version of Rojas's play (all twelve acts) in Spanish.

Rossetti, Christina

Christina Rossetti Overview
http://www.stg.brown.edu/projects/hypertext/landow/victorian/crossetti/
crov2.html
   Part of the *Victorian Web.*

Rossetti, Dante Gabriel

***Rossetti Archive, The*
http://jefferson.village.virginia.edu/rossetti/rossetti.html
   Writings and paintings of Dante Gabriel Rossetti; a hypermedia research
   archive sponsored by the Institute for Advanced Technology in the Humanities; not yet complete, but demonstrating the archive design.

Rousseau, Jean Jacques

Jean Jacques Rousseau Association
http://www.wabash.edu/rousseau/
   Short, simple home page with links to brief biographies of Rousseau,
   music he composed, images of Rousseau and his world, and other sites
   related to him.

Rulfo, Juan

Arts and History—Juan Rulfo
http://www.arts-history.mx/rulfo/rulfo2.html
   Page on the *Virtual Forum of Mexican Culture* site; links to several strik-
   ing photographs by Rulfo, accompanied by badly translated text.

Sartre, Jean-Paul

Existentialism Jean-Paul Sartre by Katharena Eiermann
http://members.aol.com/KatharenaE/private/Philo/Sartre/sartre.html
   Tribute page in the context of an existentialism site; links to Sartre biography, random passages from his works, and essays and reviews about
   the philosopher and his thought.

Schwartz, Delmore

Valencia West LRC—Schwartz, Delmore
http://valencia.cc.fl.us/stage/wecstage/lrcwest/schwartz.html
   Brief bibliography for study of Schwartz's life and work; a study guide
   for undergraduates at Valencia Community College.

Second Shepherd's Play, The

HIEU 826 Seminar Paper
http://members.tripod.com/~Dante_6/bibles.htm
> Paper entitled "The Literary Boom: Forms of Early Religious Vernacular Texts in England (c. 1475–1570)," written in 1993 by a graduate student at the University of Virginia; touches on *Second Shepherd*, but mainly supplies context.

Note on Dialect (Second Shepherds' Play)
http://icg.fas.harvard.edu/~laa14/dialect1.html
> Analysis of "the King's English" in the *Second Shepherd's Play*; a Harvard University site.

Shakespeare, William
With the exception of the starred sites, most of the sources listed below are average or below; they have been included to illustrate the range of the thousands of literary websites dealing with Shakespeare.

**Best Sites
http://daphne.palomar.edu/shakespeare/bestsites.htm
> The best of Palomar's exceptional site: "Mr. William Shakespeare and the Internet"; important selection of helpful sites, chosen from the enormous (mostly worthless) glut of Shakespeare websites.

**Complete Works of William Shakespeare, The
http://the-tech.mit.edu/Shakespeare/works.html
> All Shakespeare's works in e-text versions based on the Moby Shakespeare; reviewed in *Choice*.

Is Shakespeare Dead?
http://www.lm.com/~joseph/shake.html
> Series of chapters from Mark Twain's autobiography, dealing somewhat humorously with the facts of Shakespeare's life, as then known; one of the chapters is presented as an essay called "Is Shakespeare Dead?"

**Mr. William Shakespeare and the Internet
http://daphne.palomar.edu/shakespeare/
> *Argus Clearinghouse* links site that attempts to be a complete annotated guide to the scholarly Shakespearean resources available on the Internet and to present new Shakespeare material unavailable elsewhere on the net.

Paper on Shakespeare's Othello
http://www.io.com/~jlockett/Grist/English/othello.html
> Simply a paper entitled " 'That Which Heaven Hath Forbid the Ottomites': The Turks in Shakespeare's *Othello*"; when accessed through URL, no author is named and the context cannot be identified.

Renaissance Texts Research Centre: Shakespeare and the Globe
http://www.rdg.ac.uk/globe/
> Guide to Shakespeare's Globe Theatre, performance schedules, news, practical information; primarily a tourist site.

Ren Faire: Elizabethan Accents
http://www.renfaire.com/Language/index.html
> Information about proper Elizabethan accents compiled for the benefit of participants in Renaissance faires, but advertised as "suitable for the scholar."

Shakespeare and Anti-Semitism: The Question of Shylock
http://www.geocities.com/Athens/Acropolis/7221/
> A lecture delivered by Grant Stirling, teacher of undergraduates at York University in Toronto; links within the text itself and to general Shakespearean sources.

Shakespearean Homework Helper
http://hometown.aol.com/liadona2/shakespeare.html
> Unusual fan site at which the author promises guidance for students who need to learn about Shakespeare resources for their homework; complete with a disclaimer addressed to parents.

Shakespearean Insulter
http://www.pangloss.com/seidel/Shaker/index.html?
> Series of insults taken from Shakespeare's plays, accessed by clicking a box labeled "Insult me again"; part of a rather maniacal series of interactive programs called Circadian Bliss; nerdish and quirky.

Shakespeare Birthplace Trust, Stratford-on-Avon
http://www.stratford.co.uk/birthplace/
> Straightforward tourist site.

Shakespeare in Connotations
http://anglisti.uni-muenster.de/conn/shakespe.htm
> Complete list (linked) of more than fifty contributions on Shakespeare in *Connotations: A Journal for Critical Debate,* mostly available on online.

Shakespeare Word Frequency Lists
http://www.mta.link75.org/curriculum/english/shake/
> Word frequency lists for three of Shakespeare's tragedies, compiled by English students at Mt. Ararat High School.

Venus and Adonis
http://www.ludweb.com/poetry/venus/
> Beautiful site on Shakespeare's narrative mythological poem, with images of paintings, sculptures, and illustrations inspired by the story.

Shaw, George Bernard

Complete Shavian, The
http://members.aol.com/tehart/index.html
  Site constructed by a fan whose dissertation and master's thesis, both included, dealt with Shaw in relation to evolutionary theory in the nineteenth century; links to other sources.

EducETH-Shaw,GeorgeBernard
http://educeth.ethz.ch/english/readinglist/shaw,georgebernard.html
  Biographical sketch and a large variety of links in the context of an education-oriented site.

Shelley, Mary

Mary Wollstonecraft Shelley Chronology & Resource Site
http://www.english.udel.edu/swilson/mws/mws.html
  Part of *Romantic Circles* website; Shelley chronology, reviews, bibliography, and other sites.

Shelley, Percy Bysshe

Shelley, Percy Bysshe. 1901. Complete Poetical Works.
http://www.columbia.edu/acis/bartleby/shelley/
  E-texts; part of the Bartleby Archive.

Sidney, Sir Philip

Sir Philip Sidney (1554–1586)
http://www.luminarium.org/renlit/sidney.htm
  Part of the *Luminarium* site.

Sir Gawain and The Green Knight

**Camelot Project at the University of Rochester, The
http://www.lib.rochester.edu/camelot/cphome.stm
  Project designed to make available in electronic format a database of Arthurian texts, images, bibliographies, and basic information; sponsored by the University of Rochester, with many scholars contributing.

Gawain (ca. 1375)
http://www.mala.bc.ca/~mcneil/gawain.htm
  Malaspina Great Books links page.

Sir Gawain and the Green Knight
http://www.luminarium.org/medlit/gawain.htm
  Part of the *Anthology of Middle English Literature* on the *Luminarium*

site; links to introduction, online resources, essays and articles, bookstore, and e-texts.

Song of Roland, The

Song of Roland, The (DL SunSITE)
http://sunsite.berkeley.edu/OMACL/Roland/
  Site provided by Berkeley Digital Library Sunsite; links to e-text.

Sophocles

Perseus Encyclopedia Sophocles
http://hydra.perseus.tufts.edu/cgi-bin/text?lookup=encyclopedia+Sophocles
  Biography, bibliography, and extensive links provided by the *Perseus
  Project Encyclopedia.*

Spender, Sir Stephen

Spender, Sir Stephen Harold
http://encarta.msn.com/find/concise/default.asp?vs=x97&la=na&ty=1&vo=
13&ti=02465000
  Entry in Encarta online, an abridged version of the CD-ROM encyclopedia; links to related subjects and to additional web-searching resources.

Spenser, Edmund

Edmund Spenser (1552–1599)
http://www.luminarium.org/renlit/spenser.htm
  Part of the *Luminarium* site.

Edmund Spenser Home Page
http://darkwing.uoregon.edu/~rbear/
  Page that attempts to connect to any and all Internet sites relating to
  Spenser; part of Renascence Editions at the University of Oregon; edited
  by Richard Bear.

Stafford, William

Amy Munno's William Stafford Page
http://www.webspan.net/~amunno/stafford.html
  Fan page with a very brief biography and one poem; part of a casual site
  called Amy's Hodgepodge.

Steinbeck, John

**ACCESS INDIANA TLC Guide to John Steinbeck
http://tlc.ai.org/steinidx.htm

The ACCESS INDIANA Teaching and Learning Center's large collection of Steinbeck resources, including everything from very general resources to particular links for individual novels: probably all the Internet data about Steinbeck lies within one click from this guide.

Sterne, Laurence

Laurence Sterne in Cyberspace
http://www.gifu-u.ac.jp/~masaru/Sterne_on_the_Net.html
Links to hypertext versions of Sterne's works, bibliography, books, journals (including numbers of *The Shandean*, an international scholarly journal published by the Laurence Sterne Trust), and essays.

Stevens, Wallace

Wallace Stevens
http://www.english.upenn.edu/~afilreis/88/stevens-poems.html
Stevens site with links to e-texts of a few of his poems and a connection to all the *Oxford English Dictionary* entries in which he is quoted; maintained by the English Department of the University of Pennsylvania.

Stowe, Harriet Beecher

Harriet Beecher Stowe
http://lonestar.texas.net/~kwells/stowe1.htm
Stowe home page with links to bibliography, information about *Uncle Tom's Cabin*, criticism, and a links page (that is correct: links to a links page!).

Strindberg, August

August Strindberg Drawings
http://www.extrapris.com/drawing.html
Mostly images of Strindberg drawings (some scurrilous), with links to other sites about him; evidently presented by a Scandinavian fan.

Swift, Jonathan

Jonathan Swift (1667–1745)
http://www.mala.bc.ca/~mcneil/swift.htm
    Malaspina Great Books links page.

****Jonathan Swift—Gulliver's Travels—Home Page*
http://www.jaffebros.com/lee/gulliver/
Elaborate, attractive home page for *Gulliver's Travels*; many links for Swift; e-text; images; rare books connections.

Tennyson, Alfred, Lord

Tennyson Page, The
http://charon.sfsu.edu/TENNYSON/tennyson.html
> Fan page with many links and quirks; maintained by Arthur Chandler of San Francisco University.

Thackeray, William Makepeace

William Makepeace Thackeray: A Brief Biography
http://www.stg.brown.edu/projects/hypertext/landow/victorian/wmt/
wmtbio.html
> Elaborate (for the Internet) biographical sketch, with brief bibliography, by Robert Fletcher, assistant professor at West Chester University; part of the *Victorian Web.*

Thomas, Dylan

Dylan Thomas
http://www.mindspring.com/~stewarts/thomas.htm
> Fan page with a few links, a breezy style, and a repugnant e-mail logo.

New Dylan Thomas Page
http://pcug.org.au/~wwhatman/dylan_thomas.html
> Australian fan site; very relaxed, but with links.

Thomson, James

Selected Poetry of James Thomson (1700–1748)
http://library.utoronto.ca/www/utel/rp/authors/thomson.html
> Part of the poetry e-text collection of the English Department of the University of Toronto.

Thoreau, Henry David

**Writings of Henry D. Thoreau, The: Main Page
http://www.library.ucsb.edu/depts/thoreau/
> Major, extensive, definitive source for Thoreau's writings, many of which have not appeared in print before; many links; sponsored by the NEH.

Tirso de Molina

Tirso de Molina
http://encarta.msn.com/index/concise/0vol10/01e43000.asp
> Entry in *Encarta* online, an abridged version of the CD-ROM encyclopedia; links to related subjects and to additional web searching resources.

Tolkien, J. R. R.

J. R. R. Tolkien Information Page, The
http://www.csclub.uwaterloo.ca/u/relipper/tolkien/rootpage.html
   Fan site with links to what must be the longest list of fan sites for any author on the Internet; dozens of other links as well: to organizations,
   music, online texts, linguistics, graphics, games, mailing lists, you name it.

Tolstoy, Leo

Tolstoy Library
http://www.tolstoy.org/
   Site dedicated to collecting and disseminating e-texts about Tolstoy's life
   and works.

Tolstoy on Christianity
http://www.signature.pair.com/letters/nov96/tolstoytoyouth.html
   Tolstoy letter reprinted in *Letters Magazine*, an online publication devoted to historic correspondence.

Traherne, Thomas

Selected Poetry of Thomas Traherne
\http://www.library.utoronto.ca/www/utel/rp/authors/traherne.html
   Part of the *Poetry On-line* site presented by the English Department of
   the University of Toronto.

Trollope, Anthony

Anthony Trollope: An Overview
http://www.stg.brown.edu/projects/hypertext/landow/victorian/trollope/
trollopeov.html
   Remarkable collection of Trollope links, including connections to Victorianism, nineteenth-century science, and the Trollope Society; part of the
   Victorian Web.

Troyes, Chretien de

*Project Gutenberg—Catalog by Author—Chretien, de Troyes,
circa 1135–1183*
http://promo.net/pg/_authors/chretien_de_troyes_circa_.html
   E-texts of Troyes's romances available on *Project Gutenberg.*

Twain, Mark

Mark Twain—Welcome from The Mining Co.
http://marktwain.miningco.com/

Mining Co. guide by Jim Zwick; very wide range of links to Twain resources on the web, including images, e-texts, guides, and a chatroom.

Unamuno, Miguel de

Miguel Unamuno
http://www.kirjasto.sci.fi/unamuno.htm
Biography and bibliography on a fan site that seems to come from Finland.

Vallejo, César

César Vallejo
http://www.blythe.org/peru-pcp/newflag/nf9801/vallej.htm
Home page for Vallejo, with a commentary, some translated poems, and a few images; presented by *New Flag Magazine*.

Vaughan, Henry

Henry Vaughan (1621–1695)
http://www.luminarium.org/sevenlit/vaughan/
Part of *Luminarium*'s *Early 17th Century* site.

Verlaine, Paul

Total Eclipse—Synopsis
http://www.flf.com/total/synopsis.htm
Synopsis of *Total Eclipse*, a film detailing the supposed relationship between Verlaine and Arthur Rimbaud.

Verne, Jules

****Zvi Har'El's Jules Verne Collection*
http://www.math.technion.ac.il/~rl/JulesVerne/
Comprehensive collection of e-text in French and English, scholarly articles, bibliography, illustrations, and links to related sources.

Virgil

Virgil Home Page, The
http://www.dc.peachnet.edu/~shale/humanities/literature/world_literature/virgil.html
Links page for Virgil; leads to dozens of sites, including texts, other Virgil web pages, bibliographies, essays, background material, listservs, chatrooms.

Voltaire, François Marie Arouet de

Voltaire Foundation
http://www.voltaire.ox.ac.uk/aa.index.html
    Home page of the foundation, based in Oxford, with links to many resources, most of which are in French, a few in English.

Walker, Alice

***Anniina's Alice Walker Page*
http://www.luminarium.org/contemporary/alicew/
    Walker home page with a variety of links, much more numerous than usual for contemporary writers; biography, criticism, reviews, interviews, and e-texts; extraordinary range; part of *Books Online* site maintained by Anniina Jokinen.

Welty, Eudora

Eudora Welty Newsletter
http://arachnid.gsu.edu/~wwweng/ewn/
    Description of newsletter; links to biography, bibliography, and frequently asked questions.

Wharton, Edith

Edith Wharton: Her Literature and Politics
http://www.colorado.edu/Greeks/aoii/wharton/wharton.html
    Site emphasizing Wharton's political views with links to political theory, bibliography, and related sources.

Wheatley, Phyllis

Diversity and Phyllis Wheatley
http://www.pbs.org/ktca/liberty/chronicle/diversity-phyllisw.html
    Some biographical information about Wheatley on the "Liberty!" site sponsored by *PBS On-line*.

Whitman, Walt

Walt Whitman Home Page
http://rs6.loc.gov/wwhome.html
    Library of Congress site, featuring recovered Whitman notebooks from the Thomas Biggs Harned Collection.

***Whitman Hypertext Archive, The*
http://jefferson.village.virginia.edu/whitman/intros/index.html
    Extensive hypertext archive of Whitman's work, nineteenth century reviews, photographs of Whitman, and teaching units; supported by the

Institute of Advanced Technology in the Humanities; by Ken Price and Ed Folsom.

Wilde, Oscar

Oscariana
http://www.jonno.com/oscariana/index.html
   Life and times of Oscar Wilde site maintained by the Oscariana Bookstore.

Wild Wilde Web, The: Welcome
http://www.anomtec.com/oscarwilde/
   Designed as an educational and entertainment site, with Wilde's wit providing the entertainment; links to biography, bibliography, and quotations.

Williams, Tennessee

Tennessee Williams on the Web Photo Gallery
http://ils.unc.edu/~mauer/williams/gallery.html
   Image site featuring photos of Williams, his family, and friends plus stills from productions of his works.

Williams, William Carlos

Williams, William Carlos
http://endeavor.med.nyu.edu/lit-med/lit-med-db/webdocs/webauthors/williams90-au-.html
   Part of the *Medical Humanities* site.

Wilson, August

August Wilson
http://www.bridgesweb.com/wilson.html
   Site in the African American Theatre series with artist biographies and play overviews; bibliography of criticism.

Wilson, Harriet E. Adams

Voices from the Gaps: Harriet E. Adams Wilson
http://www-engl.cla.umn.edu/lkd/vfg/Authors/HarrietE.AdamsWilson
   Biography, selected bibliography, and related links for Wilson in series on Women Writers of Color; researched by Karen Marie Woods, English Ph.D. candidate at the University of Minnesota, where the site is maintained.

Woolf, Virginia

Virginia Woolf Web
http://www.aianet.or.jp/~orlando/VWW/
> Home page of the Virginia Woolf Society of Great Britain with links to the Quentin Bell Memorial that lists dozens of Bloomsbury-related sites.

Wordsworth, William

Lake Poets, The
http://www.globalnet.co.uk/~burge01/page52.htm
> British fan site devoted to links for Wordsworth and Coleridge.

Links to Wordsworth-Related Material on the Web
http://members.aol.com/wordspage/links.htm
> Convenient collection of links to a wide range of Wordsworth resources, including images, online journals, and e-texts.

TCG's Wordsworth Page
http://www.usd.edu/~tgannon/words.html
> Fan page with a great many links, a totally unscholarly tone, and a "Wordsworth Quote of the Moment" function that helps to trivialize the whole site.

Wordsworth, William. Complete Poetical Works.
http://www.cc.columbia.edu/acis/bartleby/wordsworth/ww991.html
> Bartleby Archives e-text version of the 1888 edition of Wordsworth's works.

Wyatt, Sir Thomas

Sir Thomas Wyatt, the Elder (1503–1542)
http://www.luminarium.org/renlit/wyatt.htm
> Part of the *Luminarium* site.

Yeats, William Butler

William Butler Yeats & the Irish Literary Renaissance
http://www.lm.com/~kaydee/irish.html
> Work in progress by Kathleen V. Donnelly, whose dissertation deals with the Irish literary Renaissance; running commentary with many links, mostly biographical and cultural; a few images.

York Cycle of Mystery Plays

Samples from 'The Passion'
http://www.schoolshows.demon.co.uk/mystery.htm

Excerpts from "The Passion"; link to FTP site with the whole play; part of the School Show Page from the United Kingdom.

Zola, Emile

Zola, Emile (1840–1902)
http://valencia.cc.fl.us/lrcwest/zola.html
General bibliography on Zola; part of a very large list of author bibliographies prepared for students at Valencia Community College.

CHAPTER 6

Evaluation of Sites

INTRODUCTION

If, as we suggested in Chapter 1, the Internet is a kind of library, it is a library without a staff, with no trained librarians to make selections, impose standards, maintain materials, or shelve sites according to topic or type. Each day hundreds, maybe thousands, of people enter this library and make changes to the collection, adding, deleting, revising, or moving sites.

The democratic nature of the Internet is widely acknowledged and often deplored because it makes evaluation a skill every user must know, practice, and constantly fine-tune. Some who lament the huge number of poor sites call for filters, selective search engines, or juried webs. These users would just as soon have someone else sort and sift. Such evaluation services are already available, and more will probably appear. In fact, many predict that the Internet as a democratic venue will give way to some kind—corporate, governmental, academic, economic—of controls. These worries, hopes, and trends notwithstanding, for the foreseeable future serious Internet users should become expert at evaluating sites and materials.

REMINDERS

First, we should remember that not all Internet material needs to be evaluated. Automated library catalogs, government publications, congressional reports, census data, and bibliographic databases such as *MLA Online* or *JSTOR* need not be evaluated, unless one is inclined to mistrust these same materials in print.

Second, evaluation requires knowing where one has landed. This requires some sense of the variety of materials one might find on websites, the range of audiences and purposes addressed by sites, and the types of web authors one may encounter. Rough mental categories—fan site, student site, teaching site, scholarly site, institutional site—are helpful for quick cataloging. Likewise, traditional research categories should be kept in mind when one is exploring a site. Does it offer primary literary texts? Are these materials readily available in print, or are they rare? Does the site offer primary sources for contextual study: contemporary reviews, journals, letters, historical material, or visual or audio material such as a painting mentioned in a novel or a poet reading her own work? Does the site offer secondary sources: criticism, history, biography, or bibliography? Simple sites reveal their wealth with only a little probing, but sophisticated sites may have hundreds of pages, and only extensive investigation uncovers everything they have to offer.

Finally, to evaluate Internet sites is, inevitably, to apply conventional standards. Sites with factual errors, outrageous claims, or no scholarly pedigree may fare poorly by the criteria outlined here. Indeed, the standards we will discuss in this chapter are inevitably conservative and safe. To apply them is to risk losing some of the benefits of the Internet, the diverse perspectives, new ideas, and unconventional interpretations. Even though a site may fail to meet one or many of the criteria below, it still may be valuable.

1. BASIC STANDARDS

Since the Internet has no staff, every user must know the basic standards that librarians, copy editors, and publishers use. These are simple to state, but not always so easy to apply, since they require either knowing the subject well or looking for corroboration in an independent source, something many of us are unwilling to do because it takes time.

Is the Information Accurate?

Although errors in vetted printed material are not unknown, factual errors on fan sites and student sites are legion. Misinformation and typographical errors are common, and even though a site may be useful for an insight, a link, an idea, or a bibliographic citation, it can be dangerous to use any site lacking a very solid pedigree for factual information. Incorrect dates, wrong page numbers in a reference to a printed text, names misspelled are among the most common errors. Incomplete information can also be a problem. Three Zora Neale Hurston sites, for example, offer three different birth years, but none acknowledge that there is uncertainty about when she was born. Good print sources and good Internet sites address such details.

Is the Material Current?

Currency is more important in literary studies than many of us realize. For example, although the *American Verse Project,* sponsored by the University of Michigan Humanities Text Initiative, clearly labels the Emily Dickinson poems it has digitized as those printed in an 1891 edition, the reader is not told that punctuation and capitalization have been regularized. The site offers accurate electronic text and fully identifies what it offers. Many readers, however, need to know that these revisions, although interesting in their own right as one of the first printings of Dickinson's poems, are now dismissed as inappropriate transcriptions of Dickinson's manuscripts. Many Shakespeare plays reproduced on the Internet appear with even less information, failing to explain which version is being reproduced and why. In short, if one seeks a literary text on the web, one may want to investigate the integrity of the text itself. Does it conform to, or at least take into consideration, recent discoveries and debates in textual editing?

Sites should also provide current scholarship. Of course, criticism from years or decades ago may be excellent, useful, and relevant, but all scholarship should be clearly dated, and for novice readers headnotes that explain current trends and past debates and issues are helpful.

Is the Material Complete?

Two problems are common: incomplete information and incomplete sites. The first is often a problem with amateur sites where skimpy biographies and interpretive essays based on limited knowledge are common. A brief biography may be useful, but users should be aware that important events may be omitted (or misinterpreted) if the biography was written by someone with little expertise. The second problem is not uncommon with ambitious sites. Since many sites go public before they are finished, users should not trust menus without clicking through several layers. George Landow's *Contemporary Postcolonial and Postimperial Literature in English* site, for example, offers a tantalizing series of menus that suggest extensive coverage of a wide range of authors and subjects, but behind many menus lie empty pages. Take note: Site maps and menus may indicate what will be there in the future and not what is there now.

Is the Site Properly Documented?

Responsible sites identify authors, sponsors, and purpose. Good sites also give dates of when the site was first posted and when it was most recently revised. Many also provide e-mail addresses for suggestions, street addresses for regular correspondence, and phone numbers. Authors of headnotes, chronologies, and critical essays should be identified, and the very best sites identify who has digitized electronic versions of literary texts on the site, and by what method. Some sites devote a page to credits, information about the site, funding, and affiliations. These pages serve both as title pages in that they provide basic information necessary for citation, and often as prefaces in that they identify the goals of the site and suggest how to use it. A site with little or no documentation should be used with caution.

Is the Site Comprehensive, Expert, or Unique?

With experience, most Internet users become more discriminating, looking for and bookmarking only the best sites. Excellent sites vary in what they do well: Some are comprehensive, some are authored by experts in the field, others are rich with hard to find material, others may be good for the classroom, and still others may be useful for a particular project. In our list of literary sites in Chapters 4 and 5, we identify truly excellent sites with two stars. We star comprehensive sites such as George Landow's the *Victorian Web,* which offers an impressive array of secondary materials, and the *Walt Whitman Hypertext Archive,* which offers all versions of *Leaves of Grass* and much of Whitman's prose. We also star sites such as *Romantic Circles,* which has been developed by some of the best romantic scholars currently working. Sites such as the *Women Writers Project* at Brown University, the *Victorian Women Writers Project* at Indiana University, and *Documenting the American South* at the University of North Carolina are starred because they provide accurate, documented, and carefully proofread digital versions of rare materials. Although all these sites may not be to every user's taste—and surely there are sites that we have missed—the starred sites may serve as benchmarks when evaluating other sites.

2. TECHNOLOGICAL STANDARDS

In addition to traditional print standards, Internet material must also be evaluated for its success in making effective use of technology. The best sites allow readers new ways of working with literary material, while skillfully avoiding clumsy and unnecessary bells and whistles.

Is the Site Free of Technical Problems?

Technical problems and long waits are still common on the Internet, although good sites minimize these as much as possible. Some glitches are caused by incompatibilities. For example, a browser may be set for a font size that makes a page illegible or a table misaligned, or a site may require specific settings for optimal viewing. Other problems are caused by a lack of advanced software (plug-ins), without which some users may find they cannot fully view a site. Sites heavy with fancy graphics and other ornamentation are often slow to load, and sophisticated sites may also be slow because they offer a lot of material and are using the most advanced technology to provide genuinely innovative and useful options.

Good sites avoid technical problems by providing a simple front page that loads quickly and that allows the user to choose a simple version easily accessed by basic browsers. High-tech sites should tell users what is required to use the site, how to get the necessary software, and how to work with the site in simpler ways. The *Oxford Text Archive,* for example, provides e-text in several different formats for basic or sophisticated browsers. It also provides information about downloading advanced text-analysis software.

Finally, some glitches are caused by faulty servers. Such problems are usually beyond the control of the authors, and if the site resides on a reliable server, the problem should be solved quickly.

Do All the Links Work?

There are two kinds of links: internal links connect pages within a site and external links make connections to other sites. Both should be current and trouble free. This goal is easiest to achieve with internal links. When a site is under construction, all dead internal links should be clearly identified. Users should not have to click to discover which listings on the menu are available and which are not. Dead external links may be unavoidable, since sites move or disappear, and even regular updates may leave such errors uncorrected for several months. But too many inoperative links suggest that revisions are infrequent or that the quality of links is low.

Links are often touted as the essence of hypertext, and some enthusiasts believe that good sites have lots of links. You may find, however, that too many links can be annoying. Clicking to a new site is easy, but it is not as easy to know where one has landed, how good the new site is, and what it offers. On good sites, external links are clearly identified as such, and the links are only to relevant, good sites. Scholarly sites rarely link to student or fan sites and often do not even link to other scholarly sites except in a separate page identified as a list of related Internet resources. Sites that specialize in links, of course, should provide lots of links, but even these should be free of dead links and should make it clear if their lists are haphazard, evaluative, selective, or complete. Links—number, quality, reliability, and currency—reveal much about a site, and quality is certainly much more important than quantity.

In the near future, as extensible markup language (XML) (see Chapter 8) is adopted as the encoding standard for the Internet, good sites will offer richer linking. Multidirectional links will be common, as will links that take the reader to a specific place on another page or another site. For example, a literary site might include direct links to specific images in an online art museum's collection. The author might also annotate the link so that a visitor to the literature site would view the image from the museum and an explanation of the connection between the literary subject and the image. Judicious use of such links may soon be a marker of a site that is both technologically advanced and intellectually sound.

Is Navigation Easy?

Navigating a site can be confusing and tedious if its structure and logic are unclear. The weblike structure of Internet sites is both the glory and challenge of the hypertext environment. Good sites use the web structure to allow readers to find easily what they know they want and to stumble serendipitously upon relevant and interesting material.

Some sites make navigation easy by using a linear design. In these sites, the first menu identifies a handful of threads, each offering a simple series of pages. To follow another thread, one returns to the first page and starts down another path. On these sites, there is little cross-linking from one path to another. Other sites make extensive use of cross-links. These richly webbed sites may offer major paths, but on each page many internal links allow jumps to other pages and other paths.

Either design may work well. The simple web design is akin to traditional print methods of organizing material, so most users will find these sites easy to navigate. Site designers who opt for complex, intricately linked webs risk frustrating users who feel they never know where they are, where to find what they want, and where they are going. Some sites solve these problems by clearly labeling links, whereas others make a site map available, as a pop-up window or in a frame that remains on the screen. Others allow users to review the path they have followed, much as the browser buttons "Back" or "Go" list the pages last visited.

One exception to the rule that navigation should be clear and explicit is hypertext fiction. Many hypertext authors eschew navigational aids. Uncertainty and even a little confusion is tolerable, maybe even desirable, on these sites. Indeed, reading well-designed hypertext fiction can be a lively experience of unwitting choices and unexpected turns. Some well-designed scholarly sites may achieve this effect as well, but few students or researchers want to wander too long without knowing where they are headed.

Are Searches Easy and Effective?

Many kinds of searches are possible on the Internet. Most commonly, users comb the Internet with search engines such as *AltaVista* or *Yahoo!* Less widely used, but equally important, is the ability to search a site. Two simple searches are possible on most sites. First, each page of a site may be searched by using the "Find" button available under the Edit pull-down menu, allowing a simple search for a word or phrase in the page (file) currently displayed. This method does not search the entire site, although it may be adequate for small sites or even for searching a literary text if the entire text is presented on one page (file). Of course, texts presented as digital images cannot be searched at all, but experts hope to change this (see Chapter 8).

For large, complex sites, it is helpful to be able to search the entire site with one request. *Excite for Web Servers (EWS)* is a popular search application that many web designers add to their sites since it is free and easy to use <http://www.excite.com/navigate/home.html>. Developed by Excite, the company that offers the Internet search engine by the same name, *EWS* searches an entire site and finds exact matches. It also finds matches that do not include the search words but are deemed relevant based on a simple, invisible index the program generates. The matches are ranked according to level of agreement with the search request, and each file is not only named but described, thus rescuing the user from guessing the contents of a file from a (sometimes) cryptic file name.

Even more sophisticated searches are offered by large archives. The *Oxford Text Archive,* for example, allows full-text searching not only of each text in the database, but also of a collection of texts as selected by the user, such as all Shakespeare's plays. The archive also offers sophisticated category searching of its database, as do many archives, which means the user can specify genre, year, language, and so forth. A search of all novels published in the 1850s, for example, may yield some surprising discoveries of now little-known books, if some musty computer-literate scholar has deposited electronic versions of such novels in the archive.

Robust and rewarding searches of library collections are also possible now with user-friendly finding aids. The simplest finding aids are traditional automated library catalogs available over the Internet through a Telnet connection. At their best, finding aids are richly descriptive and fully searchable inventories. The *Online Archive of California,* a collaborative project of the University of California, Berkeley, and Sun Microsystems, offers links to excellent finding aid sites for the major university and research libraries in California. From here, one can visit the Huntington Library finding aid site, for example, and discover an impressive Jack London collection fully described, including a detailed, comprehensive list of the letters in the Huntington from London to various tramps, thieves, housewives, writers, and admirers. One can search individual collections such as the London collection or the entire library. In other words, one can easily discover if the Huntington has any letters from Jack London to Frank Norris or if the library has anything related to any other writer, famous or unknown, in any of its specialized collections. Viewing the material itself requires a trip to the Huntington Library, but reading a list of those who received London's missives is revealing and might induce a devoted fan or eager scholar to arrange a special trip to the library armed with detailed knowledge about what can be found there. In the past, one had to consult print inventories, which are expensive to buy and often hard to find in public or small college libraries. (Note: London enthusiasts who cannot visit the Huntington Library may want to visit the online *London Collection,* also part of the *Online Archive of California,* which includes digital images of manuscripts and letters at the Bancroft Library.)

Less satisfying finding aids, such as those for the Houghton Library at Harvard, may be incomplete or may be nothing more than a Telnet connection to the library's online catalog. Although access to the online catalogs of libraries such as the Houghton is helpful, the card-catalog entries do not exploit the aesthetic and technical capabilities of the Internet. Finding aids promise to be in the near future an important and powerful use of the Internet for searching library collections across the world.

Is Technology Used Appropriately?

The answer to the question of whether technology is used appropriately will vary by taste, but egregious misuses of technology are annoying to all, and good uses are truly helpful. Animated figures dancing across a front page, for example, are entertaining on a site for children, but are rarely necessary for literary sites. On the other hand, frames (a split screen in which each side operates independently), pop-up windows, and material that appears when the mouse is passed over the text (but not clicked) may allow a site to present annotations, commentary, definitions, or links without cluttering the main page. Ultimately, some viewers want simple presentations, whereas others are delighted by the tricks technology makes possible.

In debates about information and presentation, some suggest that information is more important than presentation and that all essential information should be presented in a low-tech, universally accessible way, not hidden behind high-tech tricks. Simplicity advocates note that the computer user and the web designer must have the same technologies if the user is to see what the designer creates. For example, JavaScript allows such tricks as drop-down lists for a hotlink, or layers of text and images that hide or bleed through each other. The first enhances navigation, and the latter might allow sophisticated displays of maps, texts, handwritten revisions, and other intertwined material. Neither of these tricks, however, can be displayed by Netscape 2.0, a browser many still use. Other sophisticated display options are also browser-specific, and a page dependent on Netscape-specific design elements may look very different when viewed by Explorer. Although many still hope that the Internet can be a place for easy exchange of information regardless of hardware and software differences, this goal has not yet been achieved. It is possible, then, that high-end technology will render some information invisible to some viewers. Indeed, links that are indicated by a graphic will simply not appear on a browser set to read text only. For the most part, a good web author is aware of the limits of low-level browsing and makes as much information visible to as many users as possible.

Designers who are excited by new presentation possibilities insist that web authors should feel free to use all the most advanced technologies. Advanced technology allows innovation in presentation, and some would say innovation in presentation means innovation in literary scholarship itself. The hope is that the market will catch up with new techniques. In short, some designers believe that "if you build it, they will come." If a site is good, users will come, and if there is a market demand, computer companies will develop the necessary software for viewing sophisticated sites.

Are Printing and Downloading Easy?

If we want to make extensive use of material on a site, we often want a hard copy. When the text arrives digitally on our computer screens, we can either print the material or download it onto our own computers. Most sites can be printed, usually by using the browser's print option. Problems can arise, however, if the site is not formatted to make printing easy. Pages with footnotes, pop-up windows, frames, drop-down lists, fly-over buttons, ticker-tape links, flashing text, or other sophisticated presentation may not print, or all the material may not print. Some pages will not print as text only, which leaves one waiting through the long delays involved with printing graphics. Although there is little one can do to anticipate these problems, and solutions are specific to each computer, printer, and site, good sites make printing relatively easy. Downloading can also be troublesome. For example, how will special features download into a text-only word-processing file? Again, good sites will work easily with the most commonly used software.

Some visionaries imagine all our work happening on computers and across networks such as the Internet. Indeed, some archives allow users to configure their own corpus (*Oxford Text Archive*) for searching, or their own version of a site (*Wilfred Owen Multimedia Digital Archive*), or their own vision of an artist's work room (*Rossetti Archive*). But until we can write in the margins, move from computer to computer without compatibility problems, and create our own virtual folders of scribbled notes, pages from a text, comments from a friend, and a last-minute idea scratched on the back of a grocery list, many of us will want hard copies of material we find on the Internet. For many, collecting such scraps of ideas and pieces of paper and spreading them out on a table is essential and satisfying. Easy printing and downloading accommodate such habits and suggest that a site is responsive to the needs of readers, writers, teachers, students, and scholars who work in a wide variety of ways on an infinite number of projects.

3. AESTHETIC STANDARDS

Aesthetic preferences about websites are deeply personal but often fundamental in shaping our responses. Some readers cannot read or hate to see white text on a black background. Some object to the primitive appearance of plain ASCII text, whereas others scoff at sites that mix lots of font styles, sizes, and colors as the "ransom note" approach to design. Some users coo over a site rich with images; others complain that they take too long to load. Attitudes about literature also play a role in aesthetic evaluations. Some eschew all signs of commercialism, recoiling at flashing headlines or advertisements for software companies floating at the top of a literary site. Others celebrate the infusion of money sometimes indicated by commercial links. Some want only stately, parchment-colored backgrounds with unadorned text running uninterrupted from margin to margin, trusting that such a presentation bespeaks scholarly merit and sober respect for the serious work of literature studies. Others delight in pink, purple, and outrageous uses of color, images, fonts, links, animation, and other web design tricks as a refreshing breeze that now blows across the too-often arid land of high-brow, ivory-tower approaches to literature.

Some would insist on basic rules, but even these may seem inviolable to some and annoying to others. For example, many web design handbooks recommend that no page should be longer than what fits on a typical computer screen. This rule may make sense for some sites, but for literature sites it may mean that many texts—primary or secondary—will be divided into bite sizes that leave the reader clicking again and again to get the next installment. To those excited about hypertext this is great; it forces the reader to create her own path through the material since she has many chances to head in different directions. To others this presentation is annoyingly discontinuous, since they prefer to scroll up and down a long page.

In short, each user will develop preferences and will find these preferences shaped and challenged by innovative designers, by new technological possibilities, by the democratic nature of the Internet, by print conventions of the past, and by old and new attitudes toward literature.

4. DESCRIPTIONS AND EVALUATIONS OFFERED BY OTHERS

Although many users may become quite good at evaluating sites, evaluations by experts can help us all find the best sites and also help us develop and fine-tune our own standards.

Descriptive and Evaluative Lists

Lists are most often thought of as a way of finding sites, but many lists also offer evaluation, if only briefly. Thorough and highly discriminating lists such as *Labyrinth: Resources for Medieval Studies* are truly helpful and a pleasure to use. More general webliographies such as *Voice of the Shuttle* or Jack Lynch's *On-line Literary Resources* may offer brief descriptions on occasion and avoid unacceptable sites. More explicitly evaluative and general lists such as *Britannica Internet Guide, Malaspina,* and *Argus Clearinghouse* claim to offer links to the best sites on the web for a variety of subjects. Experienced web users and serious students of literature may be disappointed by these lists, however. *Malaspina* makes great claims about educational goals, but its pages are cluttered with flashing headlines, the list fails to include many of the best literature sites, and too often it offers nothing more than a list of links to online stores (*Amazon.com*) or databases of electronic texts. The sites for William Wordsworth, for example, include links to several bookstores, a highlighted link to the *Bartleby Collection* at Columbia University, and a collection of basic e-text, but not a sophisticated site with extensive Wordsworth materials. *Malaspina* does not list the *Romantic Circles* site or several other useful sites on Wordsworth. *Argus Clearinghouse* claims to be the Internet's premier research library, but it offers only a handful of literary sites. *Britannica's Internet Guide* is an interesting, although odd and eclectic, selection of literary sites. It can be annoying to use because every page advertises for the *Encyclopedia Britannica Online* and the lists of literary sites are buried deep. Moreover, the star ratings are unreliable: thorough, scholarly sites may receive the same single star evaluation as skimpy sites. Nevertheless, by searching the site one may find material overlooked in Lynch's list, *The Voice of the Shuttle,* and other literary webliographies.

Published Reviews of Sites

Reviews of websites will, many hope, become a reliable way of identifying good sites. To date, however, reviews in print scholarly journals are rare. No specialized scholarly journal regularly reviews websites, although several have published articles on relevant Internet resources. A guide to Arthurian Internet resources appeared in *Arthuriana,* for example, and *American Studies International* and *Victorian Institute Journal* have also published such essays. *PMLA* (a journal of the Modern Language Association) has some Internet reporting in a feature called "Internet News" which announces and solicits contributions to websites. A few other journals and institutions are also showing signs of awakening interest.

Some online journals identify Internet resources. *Postmodern Culture,* the oldest electronic journal, offers a list of postmodern studies, and *American Quarterly* is currently developing an online version with articles on scholarly electronic projects, including websites. *Romanticism on the Net,* a peer-reviewed electronic journal, also includes links to Romanticism Internet resources.

Educational journals, Internet magazines, and other glossy news magazines also occasionally identify a worthy literature site. The primary sources for offline Internet reviews are library journals, such as *College and Research Libraries News* and especially *Choice: Current Reviews for Academic Libraries,* published by the American Library Association. *Choice,* a periodical that has pioneered academic reviews of Internet sites, reviews print and web material in all disciplines, and since it began reviewing websites in August 1997, it has discovered and reviewed many of the best literary resources on the Internet. All its reviews of websites through 1998 are compiled in a special issue that is probably the single most helpful print source in assessing Internet resources (*CHOICE Web II: Supplement to Volume 35,* 1998). Also of interest is the regular information technology section in the *Chronicle of*

Higher Education, especially the page that identifies a noteworthy site or two in a variety of disciplines. Some computer magazines offer useful reviews. *Database: The Magazine of Electronic Research and Resources,* for example, reviews (in addition to business sites and databases) such online resources as the 1901 edition of John Bartlett's *Familiar Quotations* on Columbia University's *Project Bartleby Archive.*

Feature articles are also useful. In 1997, *Choice,* for example, published "Literature in Electronic Format: The Traditional English and American Canon," a bibliographical essay by Joanna E. Gates on literature and the Internet; her webliography, *Internet Sites for Choice Magazine,* available online, remains a useful list of good literature sites. The *Chronicle of Higher Education* featured *Romantic Circles* in a 1996 issue and the *Whitman Hypertext Archive* in a 1998 issue. Many local and national newspapers also run technology columns and features that typically review commercial sites but that may, on occasion, mention literary sites.

Hypertext fiction also lacks forums for regular reviews. The *New York Times Book Review* does not yet regularly review it, nor are such reviews easily found in other print venues. Naturally, online venues are more likely to review the new literary mode. *Postmodern Culture* regularly lists contests, awards, and notices regarding hypertext fiction, and Eastgate, a major publisher of hypertext fiction, is a good source for promotional reviews and samples of their publications.

Awards and Ratings

As with reviews, awards and ratings may become useful in the near future, but they are not yet reliable indications of a truly accurate, thorough, and worthy literature site. *Choice* identifies outstanding sites with a special citation, but no other award currently available has much meaning for the discerning web user. Not that awards are meaningless, but most are given out in very large numbers and are based less on content than on design and technology. For an impressive list of awards given to one site and links to the home page for each award-giving group, visit the awards page for *Luminarium.* A beautiful site for medieval literature, *Luminarium* lists its awards on a separate page that is itself attractive and suggestive of the range of accolades available such as "Best 2500 sites identified by PC Novice," "Surfer's Choice," and "Cool Award." Unlike *Luminarium*'s discrete list of awards on a separate page, some websites open with proud displays of blue ribbons or five gold stars. Unfortunately, many of these awards are handed out in an effort to promote a commercial site or product, with little attention to reliability and accuracy of content. In short, like the *Argus Clearinghouse* and *Britannica* lists, most awards and rating systems are too broad or inconsistent to make useful distinctions between literature sites.

Online Guides to Evaluation

Many sites offer assistance with evaluation. *Voice of the Shuttle* identifies several, including the extensive *Evaluating Web Resources* developed by the librarians at the Widener University Wolfgram Memorial Library. A more focused guide to evaluating electronic literary texts is offered by *CETH: The Center for Electronic Texts in the Humanities.*

CHAPTER 7

The Internet and Teaching

INTRODUCTION

Enthusiasts champion the Internet for the resources it makes available to students, and they celebrate hypertext as a new way of reading and writing that empowers students. The enthusiasts are not all wrong. The materials available on the Internet include images and transcriptions of rare, fragile literary documents and also extensive archives, some of which are more complete than the holdings of many college libraries on a given author, text, or period. Students can access, for example, all the contemporary reviews of Whitman's poetry, digitized images of scribal manuscripts of *Beowulf,* and posters for and reviews of Mark Twain's public lectures and performances. Historical materials that provide rich context for literary studies are also easily available. Browsing through the rapidly expanding archives of maps, photographs, and other images in the online collection of the Library of Congress provides ideas for a wide range of literary projects. Secondary sources are also now commonly available to students. Increasingly, colleges and universities subscribe to impressive databases such as *JSTOR, ProQuest,* or *Project Muse* offering online access to articles (often full text) in journals many college libraries do not collect. Resources for teachers are also extensive: syllabi, course home pages, sites linked to anthologies, and assignments for particular texts are all easily found on the Internet.

The pedagogical promise of hypertext, although more theoretical and difficult to prove, prompts excitement that is equally intense and probably equally valid. Teachers use the Internet to present course materials (syllabi, assignments, readings), and many now use electronic discussion lists to prompt conversation outside the classroom. The greatest claims, however, are for student-created web material. Enthusiasts report that students who create web projects read more widely, spend more time on their projects, and think more creatively than those completing conventional assignments. Some teachers report that students continue to update their web pages long after the course is over, and others suggest that the power of "going public" motivates students to revise more and to pay attention to creating work free of basic errors.

Of course, at some point we must end the breathless recitations of all that is available and possible and begin teaching with Internet resources and tools, discovering what insights they make possible. We must also listen carefully to candid reports about how much time the technology itself can demand (for example, teaching HTML to students or debugging a web page). We would also be wise to listen to teachers who question the revolutionary power of hypertext. They remind us that hypertext alone will not teach students to make connections, and intellectual work is often best performed and taught in the rich, broad, and flexible bandwidth of real-time human interaction in the classroom. Indeed, the advent of the Internet neither obliges us to use technology nor relieves us of the duties of teaching reading, writing, and critical thinking. There is, so far, very little formal assessment of the impact of the Internet on teaching. Testimonials and anecdotes abound, however, and there is no doubt that as colleges and universities wire classrooms, the Internet will have a significant impact on teaching literature.

This chapter begins with two basic issues, citation and plagiarism. Then, Part 1 outlines what materials are available to help a teacher design and teach a course. Part 2 surveys what texts are available and how electronic materials can be used in the classroom and in a course. Part 3 focuses on the Internet as a pedagogical tool: e-mail, discussion lists, course management software, hypertext lectures, online tutorials, and student web projects. Finally, Part 4 briefly discusses how writing teachers are using the Internet.

BASICS: CITATION AND PLAGIARISM

How do I prevent or discover plagiarism? is one of the most frequently asked teacher questions. Undoubtedly, the Internet makes plagiarism easy. Students may cut and paste sentences and paragraphs into their own papers, or they can download and print an entire essay without even reading it. Student-level essays abound on the Internet, and since these are so tempting, some sites post stern reminders to discourage plagiarism. The Internet also makes it easy to purchase a term paper: Orders can be placed and papers sent in minutes. Some plagiarism can be verified by using a metasearch engine to comb the Internet for a distinctive sentence or passage from the student's paper. Some teachers report confirming suspected plagiarism within a few minutes of searching the Internet. More sophisticated plagiarists will not be discovered as easily, however. Some English teachers now depend on in-class writing, tests, and very class-specific topics for out-of-class essays.

How do I cite an online source? is one of the most frequently asked student questions about using the Internet. The full MLA Guidelines are available in the fifth edition of the *MLA Handbook* and online at <http://www.mla.org/set_syl.htm>. The principles are simple. Include the following when available and relevant:

1. Authors or editors (last name first)
2. Title of specific page (in quotation marks)
3. Title of the site (underlined)
4. Publication information (institution and date of last update)
5. Date the site was accessed
6. The URL.

Example:

Eaves, Morris, Robert Essick, and Joseph Viscomi. *The William Blake Archive.* University of Virginia. Jan. 1999. 11 Jan. 1999. <http://jefferson.village.virginia.edu/blake/>

1. THE INTERNET AS A RESOURCE FOR TEACHING IDEAS AND MATERIALS

The Internet offers a wealth of materials for literature teachers. When developing a new course, teaching a text for the first time, or looking for fresh ideas, teachers will find syllabi, pedagogical sites, discussion lists, and helpful assignments. The amount of teaching material available on the Internet may seem daunting, but perusing such resources allows us to see how others teach. In a time when faculty lounges and leisurely conversations are rare, the Internet allows teachers to share ideas and to look over each other's shoulders.

Syllabi and Course Home Pages

The range of syllabi on the Internet is impressive. They can be found linked to the home pages of English Departments or to home pages for individual professors. The University of Texas at Austin and many other schools post syllabi regularly, and the *World Lecture Hall* is a site with hotlinks to syllabi for any subject. Links to syllabi are also available at both Alan Liu's *Voice of the Shuttle* and Jack Lynch's *On-line Resources*.

Some online syllabi are simple electronic versions of print syllabi. These offer no links to Internet sites and perhaps no commitment to using the Internet in teaching except as a way to deliver a copy of a syllabus to students who have lost the classroom handout. They may not be flashy, but syllabi that offer reading lists, useful secondary sources, or innovative approaches to grading can be precisely what one needs when approaching a new subject or when weary of one's own methods of weighing attendance and class participation, exams and essays, journals and oral presentations.

Other syllabi are technological wonders. For those interested in integrating technology, some syllabi offer impressive examples of how the Internet can be used throughout a course. These sites are more appropriately dubbed course home pages. Typically, a course home page includes syllabus, assignments, handouts, and other conventional print teaching materials. A course home page also may include descriptions of web assignments and links to required or suggested Internet sites. Some display web material developed by the teacher, which may be as simple as reprints of lectures or as extensive as fully developed sites with original material, links, images, and texts. Course home pages may include instructions to students for participating in a course electronic discussion list or for using a course chatroom. Some course home pages archive student contributions to discussion lists, which students may consult and use in their print or hypertext essays. A course home page can be used to post answers to quizzes, to allow students to view their grades (and no one else's) at any time, and even to publish course evaluations. Many course home pages also include student-authored material, sometimes small individual web projects and sometimes large collaborative projects developed over many semesters, or years, or in collaboration with students at other universities.

Pedagogical Sites and Real-time Seminars

Developed by teachers, scholars, or publishers, pedagogical sites offer materials and assignments aimed at students. The most basic pedagogical sites are teachers' websites on individual authors, texts, or topics. Some of these are lectures used in a particular course and thus may include details relevant only to the teacher, the course, and her students. Other teaching sites may be hypertext lectures such as Stuart Lee's on World War I poetry, available at the *Wilfred Owen Multimedia Digital Archive,* or comprehensive guides to a subject such as Paul P. Reuben's *PAL: Perspectives on American Literature: A Research and Reference Guide,* which offers historical summaries, links to e-text and other teaching sites, assignments, and much more. One may, of course, use sites with good primary and secondary sources developed by others or develop one's own. Sites that are essentially someone else's lecture notes will not serve most teachers since few of us are comfortable delivering a lecture we did not write. Developing one's own site can be time consuming, yet rewarding, since it will be aimed at a very specific audience and may reflect one's own research interests and scholarly expertise.

The most sophisticated pedagogical sites hyperlink a rich array of materials, primary and secondary, and ask students to make connections and move towards nuanced literary analysis. Such sites may be built by individual teachers for a specific course or developed collaboratively. Recently, the U.S. Department of Education has funded the development of Internet teaching sites on Whitman and Dickinson, and the National Endowment for the Humanities has supported the construction of a high school teaching site focused on Romanticism. The Whitman and Dickinson teaching sites are linked to hypertext archives on each poet, but they focus on a topic—"The Geographical Imagination of Whitman and Dickinson" or "Dickinson and the Santo Domingo Moment," for example—and they publish additional primary and secondary sources. Some scholarly sites publish student work, and others provide suggestions for how to use the site in the classroom.

Publishers also provide pedagogical sites on the Internet. Often keyed to textbooks, anthologies, and frequently taught novels, these sites are usually written by professors and offer excellent notes and suggested assignments. Linked, inevitably, to promotional pages, the best sites offer intelligent discussions of specific texts and ideas about how to teach the material. For several years Norton has offered such sites for free, but soon their very useful sites may be accessible only with passwords printed on the inside cover of their anthologies. The logistics of password access, given how anthologies are passed around and resold, are not yet clear, but the shift to limited access reflects publishers' efforts to use the Internet and their own pedagogical sites to sell their books.

Using Internet technology and the widespread availability of computers, some publishers also offer real-time conversations with writers. Penguin and Longman, for example, have joined together to set up online seminars with contemporary authors. The *Penguin Online Auditorium,* available to classes that use a Longman text and at least one featured Penguin novel, will allow teachers and students to participate in live, online seminars with such writers as Dorothy Allison, Julia Alvarez, Mary Karr, and Arthur Miller.

Finally, book club sites may serve as pedagogical sites. Many popular books clubs (such as Oprah Winfrey's) offer intelligent and probing questions on the novel of the week or month. Often appropriate for an undergraduate course, such sites are free of scholarly and pedagogical jargon and thus introduce students to a world outside academia that is committed to reading and thinking about literature.

Discussion Lists

Discussion lists can be good places to get help with teaching dilemmas or find new ideas. Author lists sometimes include discussions about teaching, and most accept questions about teaching strategies or about primary or secondary sources. Very specific questions are also acceptable and are usually quickly answered. In addition to author lists, there are discussion lists devoted to computers and literature and also some devoted to teaching.

Assignments

Ready-made assignments are easily available on the Internet. Most of the pedagogical sites already mentioned offer assignments, and course home pages usually include them. As noted, comprehensive sites on an author, text, period, or genre may include a section devoted to using the site in the classroom, and some have fully developed pedagogical units with additional primary material, secondary sources, and suggested topics for research, reflection, discussion, or writing assignments. Since, in some ways, assignments are easily created—although not as easily taught, explained, or graded —the assignments on the Internet are no different than the questions, topics, and suggested projects typically offered in anthologies and teaching editions. Such suggested assignments are, perhaps, most useful because they point us to rich moments in a text or archive. For example, the questions on sites linked to anthologies are helpful for thinking about how to teach an unfamiliar text for the first time. Such questions can serve as a tutorial for a teacher, indicating textual moments worth close study, and as thoughtful "faculty lounge" suggestions for good assignments. Such pedagogical material is particularly helpful when linked to a complex, scholarly site that both teacher and students may find too deep to plumb easily.

2. ONLINE TEXTS FOR TEACHING

Literature Texts

Finding e-text of canonical works published before the twentieth century is relatively easy. General searches often yield several electronic versions, and searches of such electronic text centers as those at the University of Virginia, Oxford University, and the University of Michigan yield editions created in accordance with the highest scholarly and technical standards. Noncanonical texts may also be found in these e-text centers or at specialized sites devoted to a period, an author, or a genre. *Documenting the American South,* for example, offers slave narratives that cannot be found elsewhere on the Internet, and the *Women Writers Project* at Brown University provides electronic versions of nineteenth-century texts that cannot be obtained even through interlibrary loan.

Choosing and evaluating e-texts for a course is, like choosing print editions, a complicated affair. The basic standards outlined in Chapter 6 are relevant, and some teachers will want to consider the advanced, scholarly standards for electronic editions discussed in Chapter 8. Of primary concern, however, are pedagogical issues. In ordering print editions teachers often distinguish between a Melville graduate seminar, for example, that requires the authoritative Northwestern edition of *Moby-Dick* with its extensive editorial apparatus, and an undergraduate survey course that needs only an inexpensive mass-market version. Such distinctions can also be made among electronic texts. William Blake's "Songs of Innocence and Experience" is available at *Project Gutenberg* and at the *William Blake Archive.* On the former the poems appear as raw text, without formatting, without illustrations, without editiorial explanations about which version is presented, and with occasional typographical errors. *The William Blake Archive,* on the other hand, is a complex, sophisticated scholarly site with beautiful images, complex search capabilities, and detailed information about each text. The site might confuse or overwhelm students who simply want to read the poems. Yet another option might be selections from *The Marriage of Heaven and Hell* at a teaching site such as the *Blake Multimedia Project,* where a page of Blake's illuminated manuscript is annotated with comments and questions that direct students to study closely the drawings and the text. Finally, a teacher might choose from the electronic texts available at such centers as the University of Virginia's *Electronic Text Center* and the *Oxford Text Archive.* The texts at these sites are accurate, tagged according to the most sophisticated SGML-TEI (Text Encoding Initiative) guidelines (see Chapter 8), and fully documented. The texts, easily viewable with old and new versions of most browsers as well as with sophisticated SGML software, appear on the screen without the clutter of textual scholarship and documentation. Text availability can be a problem, of course. The *Electronic Text Center* collection, for example, does not include Blake, although its holdings in American literature are extensive, while *Oxford Text Archive* includes *The Marriage of Heaven and Hell, Selected Poems,* and *The Book of Thel.*

As with print editions, electronic versions and sites appeal to different audiences and are suitable for different projects. In print, pricing usually reflects and underscores these differences, and it is likely that price will soon become an issue on the Internet. For example, as *The Complete Writings and Pictures of Dante Gabriel Rossetti: A Hypermedia Archive* is published in installments over the next few years by the University of Michigan Press, the free online site will not grow. Free sites will be teasers, or perhaps full and rich, but not the advanced, sophisticated, and comprehensive archives that publishers will promote and that will cost hundreds or thousands of dollars for annual subscriptions. As this happens, the scholarly electronic edition will become more like its print forebear. Such editions will be resources that libraries acquire, depending on their budget, and they will be used less as reading copies for courses and more for research and in-depth textual studies.

Literature E-texts in the Classroom

Using electronic texts—of any quality—in the classroom can pose logistical problems. Assigning electronic versions of short texts as an alternative to ordering collections that will be used for only one or two selections can be an attractive option. And yet, costs are passed to computer centers when students decide to print the text. In a nonwired classroom, if students arrive without a print copy, the teacher may want to project the text. For close analysis of specific passages and for short poems, a large, projected image can be quite dramatic, but students who do not have copies will not have control of the text and will not be able to search for passages they want to examine. In the wired classroom—typically such classrooms allow one station to control all the others or allow each person to work independently—some of these problems may be avoided.

Sophisticated technology classrooms, however, do not solve the awkward problem of writing in the margins of an electronic text. Many teachers encourage students to underline, annotate, and scribble on the printed page, and although technology enthusiasts acknowledge that electronic editions must include this interactive option, only rudimentary models exist so far. One option allows a teacher or student to create a personalized, annotated path through an archive. On the *Wilfred Owen Multimedia Digital Archive,* for example, a teacher might create a tutorial (or path) through the archives, which means that the teacher selects and orders the archive material and adds comments that appear in a sidebar frame alongside the manuscript image, film clip, photograph, or so forth. The path is saved on the server site of the archive itself and is then accessible by others. A teacher could create a path for students to use or assign students to create their own paths. Still, until a more supple interactive hypertext is common, electronic editions may be most useful for out-of-class study, for research projects, and for only occasional use in the classroom.

Ultimately, the Internet may change the teaching of literature simply because new material is readily available. Even if scholarly archives disappear behind the firewall of expensive subscription rates, the Internet will continue to be an impressive addition to most college and university libraries. Undoubtedly, with the availability of more texts, rare texts, manuscripts, and alternate versions, literary studies and teaching will change. As the teaching of literature has been shaped by the founding of midwestern land-grant universities open to huge numbers of the middle class, by the rise of New Criticism, by the widespread use of anthologies, and by poststructuralist theories, so the availability of more texts richly pertinent to literary studies will change the teaching of literature. How? First, authoritative and definitive texts may give way to a notion of fluid texts: On the Internet, scholars, students, teachers, or anyone can peruse many drafts and versions of a poem or novel. The perfect, unified work of art, already deconstructed and contextualized, may now become a text always in process, always in relation to other versions, to letters, and to reviews. Second, the abundance of texts may reshape the canon and the dynamics of canonformation. There will remain texts that are much discussed and others that are ignored, but the availability of so many texts may promote a decentered, flexible canon more quickly responsive to the interests of scholars, teachers, and students, and less rigid and nationalized than the canons enthroned in anthologies. Skeptics retort that the Internet has not made noncanonical texts more available. Canonical texts and authors are typically the first to be converted into electronic form; creating scholarly electronic editions and maintaining large, stable electronic text centers is expensive, and funds typically come from major universities and government agencies. Enthusiasts insist, however, that as individuals create electronic versions and as libraries convert their special holdings, noncanonical texts will come online and will be preserved since, once made, electronic editions should be inexpensive to maintain.

Primary Contextual Sources

For those teachers and students willing to explore the vast riches of historical materials online, the Internet facilitates teaching literature in its cultural context. Students will easily find (1) traditional historical documents such as treaties, speeches, court decisions, proclamations, newspapers, demographic information, and other public material; (2) documents of social history and popular culture such as letters, photographs, diaries, family records, advertising, and songs; and (3) works of art in other media such as painting, drawing, music, film, dance, architecture, and sculpture. Using this material, of course, requires finding and evaluating it, and teaching with it demands revising old assignments and creating new ones.

Searches may be performed by teachers or students. The broadest assignment, which simply asks students to find relevant contextual material, works best for adept users of the Internet. Other teachers prefer more pointed assignments such as searching a specialized collection of nineteenth-century photography from the Library of Congress or antebellum newspaper editorials collected by Furman University. These more focused searches may reduce the amount of time students spend sifting through material. Ideally, assignments require students to use what they discover. Students search further and discriminate more carefully when they must work with what they find and when they are required to make persuasive arguments for connections between historical materials and the literary text.

Evaluating historical resources depends, as with the evaluation of electronic literary material, on what one needs. The basic evaluation criteria outlined in Chapter 6 are relevant. Students and teachers will probably prefer to use sites developed by experts and institutions, since these are more likely to offer accurately dated, identified, and digitized material. At the highest levels, the standards discussed in Chapter 8 for digitizing and preserving literary texts also apply to historical resources. Indeed, historians and libraries may be devoting even more time and money than literary scholars to converting print resources since searching large databases is a research method widely used by historians. Teachers and students may be satisfied with lower standards if the goal is not in-depth historical inquiry but rather some sense of an era, a place, an event. The varied quality and purpose of sites is, perhaps, most apparent with one of the most popular topics in U.S. history, the Civil War. There are hundreds of sites: Some are large databases, some are focused studies, some are eclectic, some repeat what is well known, some are inaccurate, and some are compelling.

Teachers who want to sidestep evaluation problems may want to do all the searching and selecting themselves. On a course home page some teachers create a set of links to good sites, whereas others print copies of Internet materials for distribution in class. Alternatively, Internet material may be projected in the classroom. The logistical problems outlined above—students cannot control the material or write directly on it—still apply, but with material solely for classroom use projection can be very effective, particularly to enliven a lecture. Students are often intrigued to see the pages of the magazine that first serialized a novel, the city streets an author wandered, the woodcuts that illustrated a first edition, the painting that inspired a poem, or the peace treaty mentioned in a novel. These projected images are a dramatic improvement over anthology footnotes with descriptions or information about such contexts. In addition, projecting images is much easier than passing a book around the classroom. Of course, slides, overhead projectors, and opaque projectors have served this purpose in the past, but the Internet and a wired classroom bring together the resources of an impressive library of historical documents with sophisticated projection possibilities that surpass these older methods.

Secondary Sources

Finding journal articles through online databases is very popular with students. Available by subscription and thus primarily to those who are affiliated with academic institutions, Internet databases such as the *MLA Bibliography, JSTOR, ProQuest,* and *Project Muse* are very popular with students who may be able to search these databases even when the library is closed. In particular, students rave about those databases that offer the full text of every article and not just a citation. The appeal of full text databases is obvious. With citation databases, the student must, after producing a list of citations, consult a library catalog to find out if the school library has the journal and the specific issue. Then the student must head into the stacks to find the bound volume or microfilm reel, hoping as she trudges along with backpack and coat trailing on the floor that the article has not been ripped out or the reel misplaced. To many students, teachers, researchers, and librarians, the advantages of online full-text databases for scholarly research are impressive: On any computer linked to a subscribing network, one can search and then view, print, save to disk, or e-mail the full text of an article. No issue is ever missing or damaged, and much shelf space is saved.

There are, however, disadvantages and caveats worth noting. First, students should not presume all databases offer full-text articles for all journals indexed. *ProQuest,* for example, is a general database of over 1,200 journals, but only several hundred are full text. More importantly, the material collected in a database may not offer comprehensive coverage. The *MLA Bibliography,* although only a database of citations, is committed to providing a complete, comprehensive database of scholarship in the field, but this is not the goal of other databases. *JSTOR,* for example, provides full text of articles in journals from many disciplines, but does not cover the most recent three years; in addition, it does not index many important literary journals. *Project Muse* also offers full text, but only of the forty or so journals published by Johns Hopkins University Press. A search of the *MLA Bibliography* and *Project Muse* may have the same final result for a student—three or four full text articles—but there are important differences. The *MLA* search provides a comprehensive list that indicates the breadth of published research on the topic, whereas the database search provides immediate results—full text articles—but leaves one unaware of the range of published scholarship.

In addition to databases, the Internet offers access to other, less traditional secondary sources. First, students may find an electronic journal with useful articles. *Romanticism on the Net* and *Postmodern Culture,* for example, offer some or all of their issues free on the Internet. Second, students may look for scholarship and commentary on the best sites devoted to the topic, author, or period they are studying. Usually created by scholars in the field, these sites often include "hidden" essays; some site introductions put forward an important interpretation of a text or author, and sometimes full essays are hidden deep in a comprehensive site. Some of this material may be a reprint of a journal article or book chapter, and some of it has been written specifically for the site. Of course, caution is important. Many essays appear on the Internet without going through any external review. An essay may be excellent or worthless, unconventional or a rehash, original or plagiarized. Third, some students may search the archives of discussion lists. These are typically open to nonsubscribers as well as subscribers, and usually they can be searched easily. Again, caution is important. This source is nontraditional: Those who post have widely varying levels of expertise and postings on a list may be thoughtful commentary, conjectures, or arrogant posturing.

3. THE INTERNET AS PEDAGOGY

Teaching Internet Skills

If we want our students to use the Internet, join an electronic discussion list, and publish on the Internet, then we will have to teach them how to evaluate sites, how to visit a chatroom, and how to create an HTML document. Within a decade, students will be learning these skills in grade school, and college librarians already often teach basic Internet skills, but some of this instruction will fall to English teachers since there are discipline-specific issues and criteria we want students to know.

With inexperienced students, the first lesson covers browsers, search engines, and standard features of web pages. Although most students surf the web for entertainment, many appreciate learning details such as how to interpret a URL, how to annotate bookmarks, how to stop a file transfer, or how to go back to previous sites visited. Students also need to know how to narrow a search with Boolean operators or with the strategies of specific search engines. Such instruction can be limited to a ten-minute introduction that ends, for example, with the students trying one "trick," such as limiting a search to edu. sites.

A more complex and more important lesson is how to distinguish between internal and external links and how to know when one is moving within a site and when one has traveled to another one. This is not always easy. For example, students may report that the *Virginia Woolf Web* includes e-text of several of her novels and stories, although this is not the case. The site provides external links to e-texts available at *Project Gutenberg,* the *Oxford Text Archive,* and other sites. The distinction is important: It is necessary for describing and evaluating the Woolf site accurately, and users must not mistakenly apply a judgment of one site to pages that belong to another. *Luminarium,* a site on medieval and Renaissance literature, is particularly good for teaching students to pay close attention to the URL for each link, since this site freely mixes, without labels or warnings, internal and external links on every page.

Evaluation is, perhaps, the most critical issue when teaching students how to use the Internet. Many teachers cover the basics of evaluating a site by teaching students to note the domain, to look for academic credentials, to beware of sites with typographical errors, to reject sites that provide no information about the site (who created it and when), and to check for documentation of primary or secondary material (date, source, and author). Many possible assignments are useful for teaching students how to find, describe, and evaluate a site, including: (1) contrast what is available on several sites on one author; (2) explore fully one site and describe what it offers; (3) find and contrast multiple electronic versions of a single literary text; (4) develop an annotated bibliography of web sites on a specific topic; and (5) outline a research project and identify appropriate Internet resources.

Many teachers use such assignments, whereas others eschew them. Yes, it is true that the Internet is full of unreliable sites and that students may naively use poor ones. Yet perhaps students do not need to spend time visiting weak sites or comparing mediocre sites to learn how to tell a good site from a bad one. We rarely ask students to sort through the material collected in used bookstores, yard sales, and thrift shops when doing research, so why should we ask them to sift through the flotsam on the Internet? There are, of course, good reasons, but directing students to the best sites may be just as effective.

If students use good sites extensively, they will learn to distinguish between deep, reliable, well-documented sites and superficial ones.

Teaching Internet skills, and evaluation in particular, may best be done by teaching with good sites, but it also requires good assignments. It is not enough just to write the URL of a sophisticated archive on the board and ask students to "read" or "visit" it, unless they are already very savvy about electronic archives. Rather, the teacher must develop assignments that enable and require students to navigate the site, find material, and "do" literary studies. Possible assignments include: (1) contrast two versions of the same text (manuscript and print, or first and revised edition); (2) search for a term in a text, such as *mulatto* in a late-nineteenth-century novel by Frances Harper, and draw conclusions; (3) summarize secondary material on a site; (4) study primary literary sources such as letters, unpublished manuscripts, journals, or reviews on a site; or (5) explain a textual editing issue as made visible in variants presented on a site. These assignments require knowledge of a site and take time to develop, but they should prompt students to interact with new literary material or with familiar material in new ways.

Teaching with Internet Technology

Many teachers are enthusiastic about how Internet communications technology itself can transform teaching. Many thus report that e-mail allows students to contact teachers easily and without the awkwardness of phone calls; others claim that electronic discussion lists allow class discussion to continue and new issues to emerge; and some claim that quiet students are more likely to speak up on discussion lists than in person. Neither discussion lists nor e-mail is real time, although quick exchanges are possible. More advanced uses of communications technology include such real-time interactions as multi-user object-oriented environments (MOOs); multiple-user dungeons (MUDs), named after the popular game Dungeons and Dragons; and Internet relay chats (IRCs). MUDs allow real-time conversations between many people, whereas MOOs allow the realtime exchange of graphics as well as text. Both are essentially chatrooms, and conversations can be anonymous, if etiquette permits. IRCs provide one-to-one conversations, like a phone call. Pedagogical uses of these technologies are many. Some teachers ask students to e-mail drafts, and others engage in frequent e-mail exchanges with every student in a class. Some teachers simply set up a chatroom or discussion list, whereas others require students to post comments regularly. If conversations are good, a teacher may require students to use online discussion materials in their essays. Some teachers direct virtual discussions themselves, identifying specific topics or asking students to brainstorm essays online, whereas others simply listen and remain an off-screen presence.

Internet technology may also be used to organize a course or to present material. In the first section of this chapter, we noted that it can be helpful to visit course home pages developed by others. For those who want to construct their own course home pages, software makes it easy. Web Course in a Box, for example, allows even novice web users to develop with ease a course home page including a syllabus, assignments, and a webliography. The software provides templates, so one need not learn HTML, and helps with setting up a discussion forum or with such advanced features as delivering self-correcting quizzes over the Internet. A course home page can become even more sophisticated with the addition of lecture notes (perhaps with additional material such as links to primary sources or to other relevant Internet sites), primary and secondary materials that will be discussed in class, and exercises, questions, study guides integrated with the lecture.

Clearly, there are many uses for a teacher-created site, but since one can spend hours simply sorting out computer logistics and glitches, it is important to ask what is achieved by putting teaching materials on the web. One answer is convenience. Students can access materials when the library is closed, when they are at home, or when they have lost a print copy. Online course materials serve the needs of distance learners, commuters, single parents, and other students who cannot easily visit a university library in the evening. Another answer is publicity. To put course materials on the Internet is to share one's teaching ideas with teachers and students everywhere. This exposure may encourage us to develop better materials, and it may contribute, albeit indirectly, to discussions about teaching. Publishing on the Internet and developing good teaching sites might also allow teachers to bring together teaching and research interests. In fact, as teachers create sites that draw on scholarly expertise and appeal to students and other teachers, there may be a genuine exchange between teaching and research. A third answer is that hypertext can allow new ways to present material. Hyperlinked material may encourage students to make connections and think in new ways because the links suggest connections without necessarily articulating them. For example, a teaching site might link poems by Yeats to his letters to Maude Gonne, to newspaper clippings about Irish nationalism, and to an excerpt from a scholarly study. The site suggests that these materials shed light on each other, leaving the student free to develop a specific interpretation.

Hypertext Assignments for Students

In addition to teacher-created sites, the Internet can be used to publish student-created sites. In fact, the pedagogical power of hypertext is, according to enthusiasts, most fully realized when students create their own web material. Possible assignments include:

1. *Webliographies.* By creating a hotlinked annotated bibliography, students learn to search, find, describe, evaluate, and compare and con-

trast sites. Webliographies also introduce them to a variety of sources and thus to a variety of interpretations, ideas, and perspectives.

2. *Hyperlinked annotations.* The teacher puts a section of a text, or an entire short text, into a hypertext forum. The students then write responses that they link to the text. Other students can read these comments and add their own. Thus, a class builds a text-based, hypertext conversation. The commentary can be scholarly annotation, brief interpretations, images, or links to other Internet material. This assignment is easiest with texts in the public domain, but getting permission to post copyrighted material is sometimes possible, especially if the text will be published not on the Internet, but on a local intranet.

3. *Student home pages.* Although a student home page is a popular assignment, on the best home pages students present not just themselves but their thinking on the course topic. They may include their essays, journals, and discussion list postings, all hyperlinked, designed, and ordered to present an intellectual identity. Some teachers report that students ask permission to update their pages even after the course is over.

4. *Web essays.* These may be simply traditional essays posted on the web for other students to read, or they may be hyperlinked to texts and criticism available on the Internet. Ideally, links should be to material that renders the argument in the essay more vivid, persuasive, complex, or thorough. Some teachers ask students to link their essays to other student essays. Thus, students read each other's papers and engage with the ideas of their peers.

5. *Web sites.* Student-created sites are usually collaborative efforts, possibly including the work of different classes over several years or the work of students at different schools. Good student sites are rich with primary and secondary sources, links, annotations, essays, and images, and they become sites that others find useful, accurate, and thoughtful.

Some teachers may despair when they first assign web projects. These assignments can take a lot of time, with much of it devoted to learning and using the technology. This problem will surely become less acute as students learn to use technology earlier and earlier in their lives. Students and teachers may also devote hours to manipulating the presentation, but this is not just pointless play. Experimenting with the appearance of a text—the layout, the margins, the font—has long been a part of presenting literary work. Poets know this, medieval manuscripts testify to it, and hypertext projects foreground it, allowing students to enter the print room, as Walt Whitman did when he published his work, and create texts in all senses of the word, verbally and visually.

The effectiveness of these assignments lies in giving students an audience beyond the teacher and in requiring students to make links and thus connections. Teachers report that students work harder and longer, research further, and create documents with fewer errors when they create Internet material. Hypertext enthusiasts also believe that reading or creating hypertext helps a student to make connections. Pope's "Rape of the Lock," for example, may be more richly understood if students are responsible for finding material to add to the poem via hyperlinks. As students track down primary and secondary texts, images, and sounds, they work closely with the poem itself and may think about what larger context is helpful for understanding Pope's text.

Although there is a lot of enthusiasm for hypertext as a pedagogical tool, there is little formal assessment. Most articles on teaching and the Internet are written by teachers who have devoted much time to integrating technology into their courses, and, not surprisingly, they tend to report success. We must remember, however, that technology itself does not teach students. The Internet may be fun for students, it may encourage some to spend more time on a project, and hypertext may allow for new ways of thinking. Yet simply because clicking from one page to another, from an Anne Bradstreet poem on marriage to an essay on seventeenth-century Puritan marital contracts, does not guarantee that a student will think about how the poem comments on marriage, law, and love. Making connections is at the heart of critical thinking, but clicking each end of a hyperlink does not mean one makes a conceptual connection between the words or images at either end. Strong students make good use of hypertext, whereas weak students may feel lost and confused. One teacher notes that it is not enough to assign a good site such as George Landow's the *Victorian Web,* or have students create their own sites. The teacher must also ask students to articulate fully the implicit connections between one page and another on a site they visit or a site they construct (Smith, 1996). In short, teachers must still teach: They must model worthy connections, and they must assist students in developing sophisticated and nuanced intellectual connections responsive to the materials gathered together on a site.

4. WRITING COURSES AND THE INTERNET

Although our focus is literature, a chapter on teaching should acknowledge the extensive work in composition and computer studies. In the 1990s, composition experts have published hundreds of books examining the advantages and disadvantages of using computers, networks, and hypertext to teach writing. The field includes practical guides for such projects as online tutoring programs and highly theorized studies that meditate on the cultural and political significance of hypertext for student writers and for the teaching of writing. Indeed, writing is now, for most people, inextricably linked to computers and Internet communications technology. For those who want further discussions about the practical and theoretical implications of this fact, there is a world of print and digital material to consult. For syllabi, the *World Lecture Hall* is useful for links to home pages of a wide assortment of composition courses that use hypertext and the Internet. For lists of recent studies, one might consult the comprehensive bibliographies of any of the books in the New Directions in Computers and Composition Studies series by Ablex Publishing. The MLA has published several volumes on composition, rhetoric, and technology, and journals such as *College Composition and Communication, Journal of Advanced Composition,* and *Computers and Composition* regularly publish articles on computers and writing instruction.

CHAPTER 8

Literary Texts and Literary Careers in the Electronic Age

INTRODUCTION

In this chapter, we focus on the technical, editorial, and professional issues raised by the use of computers to produce, distribute, preserve and study electronic texts. Part 1 explains how texts are encoded. Part 2 surveys issues and debates in scholarly electronic editing and lists the new MLA guidelines for electronic editions. Part 3 briefly discusses the issues libraries confront in developing online resources. Finally, Part 4 surveys the impact of computers on academic careers.

1. ELECTRONIC TEXTS AND ARCHIVES

Dreams

Although this section surveys the technology underlying literature pages on the Internet, it is exciting to begin with imagining all that we might want from the digital revolution. Dreaming suggests what may be possible in the near future and also encourages us to evaluate current electronic resources by what we desire rather than by what is feasible. Fantasies about what to do with computers and literature also allow us to push computer scientists, electronic editors, and others to build the hardware, software, and electronic texts, archives, and libraries that we want.

So, what might we want from a full electronic archive? First, all versions of a text should appear in a fully searchable electronic form, along with all the texts and documents (letters, journal entries, publishing records) relevant to the history of the text. We will want digital images of manuscripts and important editions or other documents and a wealth of contextual material, including explanatory notes, annotations, maps, historical documents, reviews, critical commentaries, bibliographies, and maybe even film adaptations or recordings.

The creator of an archive makes difficult decisions about its boundaries—what is and what is not relevant—and must bring intellectual integrity and vision to the collection. Once collected, however, we want this material richly linked so that hot buttons, pop-up windows, and menus allow easy access to annotations, variant texts, parallel texts, and critical commentary. The archive should be user-friendly to undergraduate students and useful to advanced scholars. We want navigational tools that allow us to wander widely and yet know where we are in relation to our own wanderings and also in relation to the structure of the entire archive. We want software that allows us to do smart searches of images and texts, to construct concordances and indexes, and to perform stylistic analyses, and we want an interactive, flexible archive that allows us to reconstruct texts, reconfigure materials, and add our own marginal notes.

Beyond our own desires to use, manipulate, and interact with the archived material, we also want a stable archive, one that will last longer than software and hardware currently last often no more than five or ten years. Indeed, we want an archive that is independent of software and hardware since no particular technology serves the interests and preferences of all. We also want archives to be accessible to many people and to be constructed with as few technical barriers as possible, and although we want interactive archives, perhaps indexed bulletin boards that encourage commentary and exchange, we also want some protection that maintains the integrity of the archive. Finally, we want to move easily from archive to archive, text to text. As we can set print copies of *King Lear, The Waste Land,* and criticism all on one desk in a traditional library, so we want to be able to compare, quote from, and juxtapose electronic texts without closing and opening different software applications.

In short, an electronic archive should achieve at least the level of accessibility, longevity, flexibility, and stability of print materials. It should also add (1) sophisticated computer tools for analysis, (2) network exchange and interactivity, and (3) increased access to virtual reproductions of rare or fragile materials.

Many barriers prevent immediate realization of this dream, including unsolved technical, legal, and economic problems. Literary texts also pose special problems because they come in many forms: verse, prose, drama, letters, manuscripts, print, live performance, print versions with hand-marked cancellations or interlineations, fragments, scribal copies, and so forth. In addition, what we do with texts varies widely: We read, teach, annotate, interpret, analyze, create concordances, edit, and republish. Some scholarship focuses on fine textual details; other studies draw broad generalizations about a collection of many texts, such as an author's oeuvre or women's writings in a particular century.

Given the variety of literary texts we study and the widely divergent questions we ask, the creation of electronic texts, archives, and libraries is not simply a task for computer scientists or computer companies. Humanities Computing, a relatively new field that encourages collaboration between scholars and computer scientists, has yielded significant successes. In general, texts can now move from machine to machine with fewer and fewer hiccups and glitches, and increasingly a text arrives in a format that allows readers, students, and scholars to use and manipulate it in old and new ways. What follows is a history of this achievement, a survey of current technological practices, and a discussion of possible future issues.

History

Scholars have been creating electronic text since the 1960s, and a reasonable guess puts the number of electronic literary texts at hundreds of thousands. Most of these were created by individuals pursuing a particular project, so these electronic texts have not been posted on web pages or packaged by publishers into CD-ROMs. Indeed, many of these electronic texts were created with specific software written just for the project. As a result, very little of the electronic material created in the past can be used easily by others.

More recently, scholars have created electronic text not to complete a particular project but as an end unto itself. As print editors create authoritative editions, critical editions, and facsimile editions, so electronic editors are now creating hypertext editions and hypermedia archives that they offer to the world. The goal is to produce texts useful to as many people and for as many projects as possible, to make text that can be read by all machines and by all software.

In the early 1990s, CD-ROMs seemed to be the most promising technology. If CD-ROMs could be read by most machines, then the textual material would be available to all. They also seemed to offer large amounts of storage space, and their contents could be accessed without the delays and interruptions of the Internet. Conveniently, CD-ROMs are also much like books: libraries can purchase, collect, and manage the disks much as they have managed print materials.

In the last few years, however, the disadvantages of CD-ROMs have become clear. CD-ROMs such as Chadwyck-Healey's *English Poetry Plus* or the *Oxford English Dictionary* offer electronic text that can only be navigated, searched, and manipulated by the software that comes on the CD-ROM. At first, this feature seemed appealing. The CD-ROM stood alone and required no additional purchases or knowledge of technology. But users now complain that they are limited to accessing and using the text in ways prescribed by the software. One recent reviewer in the *Times Literary Supplement* applauded the Shakespeare material brought together on a CD-ROM but noted that he could not manipulate the texts and commentaries as he wished, even though what he wanted to do was relatively simple. Essentially, there is no option of separating the text from the software and usually no way to use the text with other software. Instead, users find that they must spend time learning the navigational tools and software that come with each CD-ROM, which now makes CD-ROMs look cumbersome to librarians who have to provide support for users who are befuddled and frustrated by the different software on each disk.

CD-ROMs continue to be published, and standardization might solve many problems, but as the Internet becomes faster and more reliable, CD-ROMs seem less attractive. There are concerns about how long the physical object will last; damage and decay are real possibilities, and revising, correcting, or updating CD-ROMs is costly. CD-ROMs also now seem small: because scholars want to add images and audio material, CD-ROMs fill up quickly, and even text-only material that is indexed in many ways may require several CDs (Hockey, 1994). Finally, as enthusiasts champion the increased power of the reader to create and annotate his own versions of literary texts in the open world of networked hypertext, the closed world of the CD-ROM seems stodgy and static since the user can neither write to the CD-ROM nor reconfigure the material.

The move, then, is toward electronic text accessed through the Internet and readable by a wide range of software applications.

What is Electronic Text?

Electronic text is text that can be transmitted from machine to machine. The transfer of text from office to office and city to city was the purpose of the Internet when it was first established, and this purpose can still be accomplished mostly simply through File Transfer Protocol (FTP). File transferring is also what happens when we "go" to an Internet site: a file, which may include digital images and sound as well as text, is transferred from one machine to another, "downloaded" from a server where the web site is stored to your personal computer.

Electronic text is usually searchable. Searches can be as simple as a word search using the "Find" option on the tool bar at the very top of most computer screens or as nuanced as very specific searches of large databases. In all these cases, searching is a matter of using software to work with electronic text.

Electronic text is usually hypertextual: A word, phrase, or image is linked to another file (text, audio, video, or graphic). Hyperlinks allow a reader to move from page to page (file to file) within a site or across a network as large as the Internet.

How is Electronic Text Created?

Electronic versions of printed texts can be created by keyboarding. A typist enters the text, letter by letter, word by word, into a computer. This process is time consuming and thus expensive, but it does achieve a fairly high level of accuracy. Some conversion projects have the keyboarding done "offshore," in countries where labor costs are lower, whereas others depend on volunteers.

Print text can also be digitized with optical character recognition (OCR) scanners. The inexpensive scanners on sale at local computer stores create digital images and not digital (or electronic) text. There are, however, scanners that can read text. OCR scanning recognizes letters and creates an electronic text much faster than a typist sitting at a keyboard. Such scanning, however, has several problems. OCR scanning systems do poorly with material printed before the nineteenth century because of unusual fonts or letter forms, with newspapers because the print bleeds through from the other side of the page, with bibliographies because of the extensive use of italics and underlining, and with microfilm prints because of the scratches and dark marks that may be read as letters. The result is that a good deal of careful proofreading and retyping is necessary to make an OCR scan usable.

What is Plain ASCII Text?

The simple, plainest electronic text exists as American Standard Code for Information Interchange (ASCII) text files. Sometimes called vanilla text, or raw text, ASCII text appears without boldface, italics, different font styles, or sizes.

ASCII is the most widely used code for creating machine-readable text. Like all machine codes, it is binary, encoding or translating data (letters of the alphabet) into a series of zeros and ones. ASCII is a seven-bit code, which simply means that each letter or number is represented by seven digits, all zeros or ones. For example, when you tap B on a computer keyboard it is encoded for transmission to the processor as 1000010. This string of seven digits can then be sent from one computer processor to another, and thus from one machine to another, or across the Internet. The seven digits are then decoded upon output back into the capital letter B, which appears on the screen. All this happens, of course, in a fraction of a micromillisecond.

ASCII, first published in 1968, was declared an international standard (ISO 646) in 1972. In its first form, the code did not accommodate languages with characters other than those used in English or with diacritical marks. No seven-digit strings were established for Japanese characters, for example. Also, there was some political wrangling about using English as the basis for an international standard, and socialist countries objected to using the U.S. dollar sign ($) as part of the basic code. In 1991, an extended version of ASCII was created (ISO-8859-1), and the earlier version of ASCII was renamed ISO-646-US, or US-ASCII. The new version creates codes to cover the characters in other languages, although not all have standardized codes yet. The biggest computer companies support a new code, Unicode, that will have sixteen digits in each string. If it is adopted worldwide, this code will accommodate most of the world's languages, thus facilitating international exchange.

ASCII may be unfamiliar to many computer users, but it is typically an option as a format in many word-processing software programs. In programs such as Microsoft Word and WordPerfect, a user can choose an ASCII format by saving a file as "text only." One can also create ASCII text files by working in the very simple word-processing programs that often come preinstalled on many machines. These include SimpleText (for Macintosh users) or Notepad or WordPad (for Windows users). Until recently, creating or saving a document in ASCII has been the best way to make sure that the document was readable by other machines and other word-processing programs.

ASCII text is one answer to making sure that electronic text is widely available because it can be read by almost all machines and most software. Not surprisingly, ASCII is the format adopted by many of the large, unsophisticated libraries of electronic text. *Project Gutenberg,* for example, is dedicated to making the largest number of texts available to the greatest number of people, and ASCII text files serve this purpose well.

It is important to note, however, that ASCII text has no formatting, no italics, no font variation, no underlining, and no hyperlinks. The text is rendered simply in the lowercase and uppercase letters of the English alphabet with basic punctuation marks. To some, this representation flattens the text, erasing the italics a novelist has used to indicate a dream sequence or the deliberate spacing of lines and words important to many poets.

What is Markup?

Changing ASCII text into something visually more appealing, and analytically more informative, requires markup. Markup can have a profound effect on a text, and some have revised the old adage "a text is only as good as its index" to "a text is only as good as its markup."

In the world of print, markup designates how the text should appear. Traditionally, blue pencil marks on a manuscript indicate to the compositor or typesetter what fonts to use, what type size is wanted, what should be in bold or italics, what is to be raised above the line as superscript or lowered as subscript, and many other details about how characters, lines, paragraphs, stanzas, captions, or any other element should appear.

Typographical markup is essentially an aid to the reader in that it typically tells us something about the structure or meaning of the text. For example, centering indicates a title, italics in a play indicate stage directions, and extralarge type size for a headline such as MAN WALKS ON MOON shouts that this is important news.

Currently, three markup languages are widely used: hypertext markup language, standardized markup language, and extensible markup language.

Internet Markup, or What is HTML?

Hypertext markup language (HTML) is currently the markup language read by most Internet browsers. Like the blue pencil marks of print editors or the codes in word-processing programs, HTML indicates how the text should be formatted by an Internet browser and thus how the text should appear on your screen. HTML is a computer code, written in the simple language of ASCII, that indicates such visual features as italics, font, color, size, spacing, and so forth.

For example:

HTML code: Virginia Woolf's finest novel is <i>Mrs. Dalloway</i>.

On the screen: Virginia Woolf's finest novel is *Mrs. Dalloway.*

The first tag <i> shows that the text that follows should be in italics, and the second tag </i> is an "end tag," indicating the end of the italics format. The electronic text editor must mark both the beginning and the end of what is to appear in italics; if the closing tag is missing, everything after the opening tag will be in italics. In this way, tags work as containers, marking everything within the opening and closing tag. Under normal viewing, the tags are invisible, but "Page Source" in Netscape or "Source" in the pull-down "View" menu in Explorer reveals the HTML code.

Although HTML has been widely adopted and although most browsers can read and process its code, not all browsers can read all versions of HTML. In its earliest version, HTML was a relatively small collection of simple tags for basic text features such as paragraph break, italics, bold, font style, and font size. In 1994, HTML 2.0 was developed by the Internet Engineering Task Force (IETF: <http://www.ietf.org/>), an international organization dedicated to implementing international standards for the Internet, and it was widely adopted. Recently, more advanced versions have appeared, allowing web authors and electronic text editors to make web pages flashier and more supple, dynamic and sophisticated. For example, HTML tags are now used to indicate how many inches should be allowed for a left-hand margin, how a text should be aligned with an image, how a text should slide across the screen or flash in alternating colors, and how a screen should be split into frames. In short, HTML transforms an ASCII text into a web page, simple or flashy.

Unfortunately, as later versions of HTML have appeared, widespread adoption has not always followed. With each upgrade, some browsers and earlier versions of other browsers are left behind. Netscape 2.0, for example, may not read many of the tags in HTML 4.0. Default settings usually take care of such incompatibilities, but not always. Standardization is also strained by corporate bickering. When HTML 3.4 came out, for example, some companies refused to revamp their browsers to work with the new code. At the same time, the two biggest software companies have created their own tags. Both Netscape and Microsoft have introduced tags that are not supported by the other's browser. These tags (usually called extensions when not part of the standard HTML) allow web page designers to create sophisticated effects, but only if the page is viewed by the appropriate browser. For example,

Netscape introduced <BLINK> to make text flash, whereas Microsoft created <MARQUEE> to make text slide across the screen, but neither browser supports the tag created by the competing company.

The goal of HTML—the easy exchange of information—regardless of software or hardware, across the Internet, requires standardization, and HTML is, for the most part, a widely accepted standard. In fact, in 1994, the World Wide Web Consortium (W3C) <http://www.w3.org> was founded to establish HTML standards and to resolve problems. The consortium includes over 165 organizations, including such corporate giants as Netscape and Microsoft as well as other commercial organizations and academic institutions.

Literary Markup, or What is SGML?

SGML (standardized markup language) is another encoding language. (For more, see <http://www.ncsa.uiuc.edu/SDG/Software/Mosaic/WebSGML.html>.) Adopted in 1986 by the International Standards Organization as an international standard, SGML is now being used by more and more editors of electronic literary texts. Although HTML is technically a subset of SGML, the distinction between them is crucial. HTML indicates how a text should appear, whereas SGML describes the nature or structure of the text. Editors call HTML a procedural markup language. It tells the browser how the text should look (italics, bold, extra large type, colors). SGML is a descriptive markup language; it describes or categorizes the text.

SGML example	*HTML example*
<poem>	
<title> The Sick Rose</title>	<i>The Sick Rose</i>
<stanza>	<p>
<line>O Rose thou art sick.</line>	O Rose thou art sick.
<line>The invisible worm,</line>	The invisible worm,
<line>That flies in the night</line>	That flies in the night
<line>In the howling storm:</line>	In the howling storm:
</stanza>	<p>
<stanza>	
<line>Has found out thy bed</line>	Has found out thy bed
<line>Of crimson joy:</line>	Of crimson joy:
<line>And his dark secret love</line>	And his dark secret love
<line>Does thy life destroy.</line>	Does thy life destroy
</stanza>	<p>
</poem>	

This is a simple example, but it shows how HTML tags such as <p> and <br> are used to get the spacing right, whereas SGML tags describe the structure and units of the text—poem, title, stanza, and line.

SGML is attractive for two more reasons. First, it allows flexibility in formatting. Since SGML does not explain how a text should appear on the screen, formatting is achieved by style sheets that translate such textual elements as title, chapter, stanza, line, sentence, paragraph, quote, and footnote into specific font styles, size, and location on the page. SGML text may come with a style sheet, or users may create their own, customizing the appearance of the text on the screen or for printing.

Second, SGML allows literary scholars to represent the complexity of literary texts more precisely and more fully. Searches of HTML text can never focus on literary features. One cannot search for metaphors for love or for all speeches by a particular character in a novel. With SGML text, however, scholars believe that such computer-assisted analysis will be possible. A search for the word *moon* in *A Midsummer Night's Dream* might, for example, be limited to lines spoken by Bottom.

The full promise and challenge of SGML is becoming evident as scholars work on specific texts and authors. For example, two women, self-dubbed "the housewives from Arizona SGML tagging team," devoted years to tagging *Dracula*. Together they identified and encoded the speaker for every line of dialogue. They also tagged narrative structures—journal entries, newspaper articles, memos, and indirect quotes—discovering along the way that the novel is a rich maze of intertextuality. They had to make difficult, interpretive judgments also. For example, who should be identified as the speaker of a line of dialogue recorded in Jonathan Harker's journal? They also tagged pagination, paragraphs, and chapters, and they considered tagging foreign words, allusions, and quotes from other texts. As the team reports, scholars can now have "a Bakhtinian field day tracing first how the characters' actual speeches compare with one another and then how the directly-quoted speech of a character compares with that character's style of narrating" (McMillan, 1997).

Markup for Humanities Texts, or What is TEI?

The problems of encoding a literary text can be overwhelming, and the solutions are nearly infinite and thus often ad hoc and idiosyncratic. In fact, as early as 1977, electronic text experts started calling for a common encoding scheme, warning that chaos would ensue if text providers continued to invent their own schemes. Ten years later, the Text Encoding Initiative (TEI) was formed to encourage some standardization of tagging practices. Sponsors included the Association for Computers and the Humanities, the Association for Computational Linguistics, and the Association for Literary and Linguistic Computing. Funding came from such major agencies as the National Endowment for the

Humanities, the Mellon Foundation, the Commission of the European Communities, and the Social Science and Humanities Research Council of Canada. For the first two years, experts across North America and Europe worked on guidelines, a draft of which first appeared in June 1990. The next four years were devoted to discussions, revisions, and tests, and the first official version of the TEI Guidelines was issued in May 1994. The guidelines acknowledge the range of work we do with electronic texts in the humanities—scholarly editions, literary and historical analysis, electronic publishing, creation of hypertext, lexicography—and their goal to "ensure that any text that is created can be used for any number of these applications and for more, as yet not fully understood purposes" <http://www.uic.edu/orgs/tei/>.

Since SGML is a very broad framework used for such projects as U.S. Department of Defense instruction manuals for building military airplanes, the TEI was formed to standardize SGML use for the humanities. The first step was to define types of humanities documents, and the second was to develop a basic set of tags appropriate for each type. The guidelines should work for humanities texts in any language, and ideally they should serve both scholars and librarians, both those who study texts and those who collect and catalog them. The guidelines identify which features should be encoded, offering more than 400 different tags.

Inevitably, there are disputes since the TEI Guidelines make assumptions about texts. For example, the editors of the *Rossetti Archive* (University of Michigan, 1999) decided that the guidelines did not allow them to present fully and accurately Rossetti's poems and paintings, so they developed their own encoding principles (Stauffer, 1998). As the Rossetti scholars and many others acknowledge, to mark up a text is to bring some features into the foreground (and make these features searchable) and to ignore others. Editors concerned with the physical features of a rare book, for example, may be eager to include tags identifying the watermark on the paper because such details often assist in dating manuscripts. Cultural critics may be more excited about tagging references to social context, such as a reference in *Dracula* to popular nineteenth-century advertisements for tonics made from blood extracts.

The TEI Guidelines acknowledge that all markup involves interpretation and that different users will want to focus on and tag different features of a text. The guidelines allow for multiple views by allowing for multiple encodings. A simple encoding of core features is required by the guidelines, but beyond that encoders may add tags, and even the same element (a word, phrase, or sentence, for example) may be tagged differently by different encoders. Layers of encoding with a basic version at the center may be created. Readers can then view and work with the simplest version, access alternative versions that include clear explanations of what has been tagged and with what principles, or even create their own encoding scheme. The TEI hopes that this approach will resolve the tensions between standardization and detailed, user-specific encoding that serves particular needs.

The TEI Guidelines also establish what should be included in a "header" preceding the text. The header, which is useful to librarians in collecting and cataloging electronic texts, includes familiar bibliographic information such as title, author, and date as well as information about the original source (if the electronic version is based on a print source) and the encoding. In the past, many creators of electronic text have not identified the principles behind the encoding because they created the electronic versions for themselves and for their own projects. The header includes information about who created the electronic version and also a full statement of the methods and editorial principles that governed transcription and encoding. The header also includes information about revisions, since electronic text is so easily revised, and such changes need to be recorded.

Another Markup Language, or What is XML?

Extensible markup language (XML) is a simpler version of SGML. Its creators believe that it offers the ease of HTML and the extensibility of SGML, while avoiding the compatibility problems associated with the former and the mind-numbing complexities associated with the latter. It is extensible because (unlike HTML, which is limited to less than a hundred tags) it is not a fixed list of tags. Instead, like SGML, XML allows each text to be prefaced with a document type definition (DTD) in which the editor creates and defines the tags that will be used. XML also offers a much richer way to link to internal or external pages than HTML. With XML, a link may point to a precise place on another page. For example, an essay on *Romeo and Juliet* may discuss the prologue and offer a link to an XML electronic version of the play or to an XML encoded online dictionary of sixteenth-century English. The links, then, deliver only the prologue or a single definition to the reader's screen, which is much faster than waiting for the entire play or dictionary to load.

XML is a project of the World Wide Web Consortium's SGML Working Group and Editorial Review Board, which focuses less on theoretical issues and more on current and practical applications. The W3C has encouraged adoption of XML as the standard markup language for the Internet in hopes that software companies, including the corporate giants, will produce browsers, editors, and text analysis software that work with XML. The expectation is that XML will serve the needs of all: scholarly editors, web designers, and casual Internet users.

2. SCHOLARLY ELECTRONIC EDITIONS AND ELECTRONIC EDITING

Scholarly Electronic Editions

Scholarly electronic editions are fundamentally different from the electronic texts found in such collections as *Project Gutenberg*, whose founders are quite explicit in their goals: lots of texts, easily available to all, in raw ASCII form. Electronic texts in the Gutenberg collection not only have basic spelling and typographical errors (something the project directors admit to tolerating), but the texts include no headnotes that identify the print source and have no encoding for typographical format or literary structure.

Scholars who devote their lives to understanding texts are eager to work with more sophisticated resources. To produce such texts, scholarly editors collect all versions of a text, examine all documents relevant to the history of the text, establish principles for selecting among versions, and study and record the history of the text. This sounds straightforward, but the problems in scholarly editing are subtle, and solutions vary. For example, some editors construct critical editions that offer a best guess at what the author intended, relegating what seem to be errors or nonauthoritative emendations to footnotes. Other scholars reprint facsimile editions, believing that a text is best represented as an exact replica of a version that actually existed at some moment, even if that includes obvious errors or details unintended by the author. The former try to guess and reproduce some ideal text, presuming that the meaning is to be found in what the author intended, even if that can never be known with absolute certainty, whereas the latter are often interested in the history, sociology, context, and artifactual nature of texts. Scholarly editing may seem unimportant to some (debates about replicating or correcting hyphenations in *Moby-Dick* may seem trivial). But as long as we believe that meaning and form are inextricably intertwined and that all textual details may be significant, we need scholars to edit carefully and to explore fully such questions, small and large.

Electronic scholarly editing, a new field, begins with an awareness of the issues and debates in traditional print textual editing and then asks what are the implications of using computers to present, study, distribute and preserve literary texts. Many scholars are enthusiastic about the possibilities opened up by electronic archives. In particular, editors are excited about the amount of material they can make available to readers. The editors of an electronic edition of the fourteenth-century poem *Piers Plowman,* for example, plan to offer transcriptions and color images of all fifty-four extant manuscripts of the poem. This immense collection will allow the reader to decide which text to study and also to explore, if desired, such matters as the scribal tradition, medieval handwriting, or Middle English dialects, since the variations in the manuscripts reveal much about changes in letter forms, spellings, and words. Similarly, an electronic edition currently under construction of F. Scott Fitzgerald's works will include all manuscripts and typescripts and thus will allow readers to examine, without consulting complicated footnotes, the various versions and orderings Fitzgerald tried out and even published. Likewise, in a full electronic archive of *The Adventures of Huckleberry Finn,* Mark Twain fans (with just a click of the mouse) are able to read the novel with and

without the contested raftsman episode. Even scholars who have felt gener-
ously treated by academic publishers note that limits are always set because
of printing costs and that they are never free to present all versions and all relevant material. Ultimately, textual editors believe that the availability of so
much material will change literary studies. As one editor suggests, "The
beauty of full-scale, scholarly electronic editions is that students of a text will
more readily than was ever the case in print editions be able to confront textual cruxes for themselves, not merely or even primarily in order to second-
guess the editor but, rather, in order to explore the critical implications to
their own uses of the text" (Shillingsburg, 1996, 166).

Still, editions cannot include everything. Boundaries must be drawn and
readers' needs and interests anticipated. An archive that works for scholars
may befuddle a general reader. Some editors, hoping that ingenious links
and hypertextual structures will provide the best of both worlds, envision
editions that are useful to readers who simply want to read the "most authen-
tic" edition and to readers who want to examine all versions and relevant
documents. Editors also imagine layers of annotations: general notes for
general readers and specialized notes for experts. Presenting and navigating
this quantity and variety of materials pose real challenges, and even ingenious solutions will not allow electronic editions to be all things to all readers. Indeed, electronic editions, like their predecessors, will reflect the habits
and interests of the editors who create them and the interpretive community
that uses them. No edition, not even the most comprehensive electronic edition, is definitive, complete, or final. Inevitably, encoding, selection of material, and annotations will fail to attend to issues, questions, analyses that
interest future readers. Definitive print editions once did not describe the
physical appearance or cost of the originals, two details now important to
those who study the history of books and the economics of publication. Instead of completeness, then, perhaps a sense of fullness and adequacy
should be the goal of any scholarly edition. As one electronic editor suggests, both print and electronic editions can only be "justified by the data
that they make available and the scholarly work that they make possible"
(Lavagnino, 1996, 70).

Modern Language Association Guidelines for Electronic Scholarly Editions

Although no absolute principles governing the creation of scholarly electronic editions exist, the Modern Language Association (MLA) has recently
appended suggestions for electronic editions to their guidelines for print editions, guidelines that require: (1) a history of the text, its physical forms, and
editorial methods used; (2) full documentation of alterations, variants, and
problematic readings; and (3) meticulous proofreading. The guidelines for

scholarly electronic editions, currently being tested, reestablish a commitment to print standards and add the following:

1. Nonproprietary encoding should be used, which at this time means using ASCII characters (or UNICODE) and SGML encoding as guided by TEI.
2. The edition should be "self-describing," which means that the text must include prefatory material (presumably in the TEI header) that describes the text (or file as it is called in computerese), the source, the editorial principles and rationales, the encoding principles, contextual information about the editors, and so forth.
3. The edition should include the software necessary to retrieve, present, and analyze the text, or the edition should work easily with widely available software.
4. The edition should probably include digitized facsimiles of source materials (manuscripts, typescripts, first editions), and the facsimiles should be annotated and transcribed.
5. For preservation, the edition should be as independent as possible of specific software applications and specific machines, and it should be maintained, if offered on a network, on a server with strong institutional support and in a form for long-term preservation.
6. For accessibility, the edition should be easy to use, and readers should be able to add their own notes and create their own links.

(See "Guidelines for Electronic Scholarly Editions" at <http://sunsite. berkeley.edu/ MLA/guidelines.html>.)

Current Issues and Challenges in Electronic Editing

Accessibility
The most immediate problem is accessibility. At this moment, few users can access the scholarly editions now being created. Although there is some software support for reading texts tagged in SGML and for doing the sophisticated searches that SGML tagging makes possible, none of the currently popular browsers works with SGML or XML, the simpler version of SGML. Some scholarly archives make their materials available in HTML as well as SGML, but if a user wants to use the SGML edition, she will have to purchase additional software. Unfortunately, only a few companies are currently producing SGML software. The Inso corporation sells, at prices in the tens of thousands of dollars, high-end software (DynaText and DynaWeb, for example) for creating, editing, and delivering SGML or XML documents. Interleaf, a smaller company, offers Panorama Viewer <http://www.interleaf.com/Panorama/>, a browser plug-in that works with Netscape to allow a user to view, search, and

annotate SGML documents. Unfortunately, none of these programs is easy to use, and there is no software yet for Macintosh users who might want to work with texts tagged in SGML.

Tagging

Computers demand total explicitness and absolute consistency, so tagging rules should be applied without variance. Texts, however, resist such reduction. Indeed, specialists acknowledge that literary texts are the most difficult data to manipulate with computers. One current struggle with encoding literary texts in SGML (or any markup language) is the hierarchical structure of markup languages. Tagging text is like putting it into nesting boxes. A paragraph in *Dracula,* for example, may be tagged as a speech or as a journal entry, but it cannot be tagged as both. Nor can a stanza that continues from one page to another be tagged both as a single stanza and as text that appears on two different pages. In short "multiple, concurrent, or overlapping hierarchies are problematic in SGML" and "intellectually compatible goals [become] mutually exclusive options" (Pitti and Unsworth, 1998). Scholars bristle at these limitations, refusing to be told that they cannot encode all the features they deem worthy.

Current solutions are thus far awkward and unsatisfying, and many scholars are now concerned that as electronic editions are created some "data" will be tagged and some will be ignored. These decisions could have long-term consequences. As some scholars have noted, SGML tagging as directed by the TEI Guidelines values linguistic details over artifactual details. For example, tags will identify who speaks which lines but not details about the physical object, such as the watermarks on a page or the smudges on a first edition. Given the time and expense involved in creating scholarly electronic editions, editors want to resist either–or decisions and develop instead tagging principles more responsive to the needs and desires of literary scholars of all stripes. Editors acknowledge that any edition will eventually become obsolete, but they want to make sure that editions constructed now "capture" and render usable as much information about the text as possible.

Links

Scholars also lament limitations in hypertext as currently provided by the Internet. Internet links typically take us from a highlighted phrase to a new page, either within the same site or on a new site. Many hypertext enthusiasts want other linking possibilities, believing that more precise and richer links will make hypertext a more supple, responsive environment for working with literature. For example, George Landow suggests that a link should be able to take a reader to a specific place on another page. This kind of link requires the web author to think more carefully about the purpose of a link, and it directs the reader more precisely, although the user may still wander around on the new page. Another kind of link, a one-to-many link, allows the reader more choice. When coupled with a link menu, a one-to-many link allows a reader to click on a highlighted phrase, view a menu of various links, and then make a selection. Still another kind of link identifies in advance what kind of information will be provided. For example, all words highlighted in red might be linked to definitions, words highlighted in blue might be links to critical commentary, and words in orange might be links to other literary texts by the same author.

Hypertext specialists also call for more flexibility in the presentation of links. With most browsers, links appear as highlighted text. Some readers find this distracting. For example, the excessively linked *Pride and Prejudice* available on the *Republic of Pemberley* site tempts us to click again and again just to see what a link yields. Invisible links that we find only when we mouse over the text or that become visible in the text or in a sidebar when we choose are some solutions now being developed. The Internet does routinely provide interactive or data-exchange links that are generated by the user. These are the links that allow us to search the *Internet Movie Database* or to order books from *Amazon.com.* Such links allow the user to interact with the site and when used with literary sites may allow for genuine interaction with extensive literary archives. Ultimately, interactive links may allow users to annotate and customize a site that would then be saved on one's own hard drive or on a server.

Images

Many scholars are eager to provide representations of manuscripts and relevant visual material (paintings, drawings, photographs). Manuscripts can be revealing documents, and electronic scholars wax eloquent about the implications of easily available archives of digitized images of complete manuscripts. Indeed, to see the heavily marked, revised, or decorated manuscripts of Joyce, T. S. Eliot, or Dickinson is to encounter texts in a very different form than we usually see them. For some readers these images are fascinating, even inspiring, and for others manuscripts are profoundly important for understanding a text. The digitized image is particularly important for understanding texts written before the age of print and, for that matter, any text in which the author has consciously shaped the appearance of the words on a page. Studying *Beowulf* as it was recorded by scribes, for example, is a very different experience than reading a paperback print edition. Similarly, digital images of manuscripts allow us to see how William Carlos Williams used a typewriter to experiment with alignment and spacing to create meaning, rhythm, and rhyme.

Digital reproductions also allow fragile materials to be consulted by more readers without endangering the original. Indeed, some editors suggest that digital reproductions can reveal even more than hands-on study of a manuscript. Recently, a Kontron digital camera copy of a charred Magna Carta revealed script that was previously indecipherable, even with the most advanced forensic photography and lighting. Editors working on an electronic edition of Thomas Hardy likewise insist that they find that a Kontron digital image of a Hardy manuscript reveals more than we can see with the naked eye. The editors of the *Electronic Beowulf* advance the same argument, although they also acknowledge that computers cannot yet handle the huge files created by such high-resolution digital images.

Editors are working to make images searchable. The editors of the *William Blake Archive* are indexing and annotating every identifiable object in Blake's paintings and illuminated manuscripts, every angel, dove, plant, hand raised, or hand lowered. Editors of medieval texts hope to make it possible to use the cursor to circle a word or letter in an image of a manuscript and then search for other occurrences of the letter or word in a handwriting style that is essentially the same.

Scholars also want digital images of manuscripts to be hypertextual, to link to other materials. Some have created virtual overlays for digital images that allow the user to move the cursor over the image and find hyperlinked buttons. Clicking on the button may produce a pop-up window with annotation, with commentary, with multiple and disagreeing commentary. If the image is of a manuscript, the button may be a link to a transcription or to another manuscript version of the same text.

Audio and Video

To date, audio and video files move across the Internet slowly and awkwardly. Some of the problems will be solved as browsers are updated and software for handling audio and video material is standardized and integrated into all browsers. Music and film specialists, like literary scholars, are also working on more sophisticated problems. They too want their materials to be searchable and linkable, which would then allow video and audio files to be integrated fully into a literary site.

3. DIGITAL LIBRARIES

Traditionally, libraries have been places where texts can be read and studied side by side. To offer the same service, libraries now must provide access to digital texts as well as print texts, in part because some texts exist only in the virtual world of the Internet. Thus, libraries have begun building and maintaining digital collections. A digital collection may take many forms. The simplest is what is freely available on the Internet. To offer this collection a library need only set up a few computers for its patrons and offer assistance with browsing and searching. Although a library has no control over this collection, most libraries see access to these resources as an appropriate service.

Other institutions, including many college libraries, also offer their own annotated, evaluative lists of web sites. This kind of collection, of course, is subject to all the vagaries that any list of web sites suffers—sites will disappear, move, or change—but such a list provides the traditional library service of judicious selection of good resources.

Libraries may also build collections of subscriptions and licenses to digital databases and materials. Most college libraries now pay annual subscription rates for access to online databases such as the *MLA Bibliography, JSTOR, Project Muse,* and others. In addition, publishers large and small are selling libraries subscriptions to reference works, literary archives, and massive collections. For example, a single reference work such as the *Johns Hopkins Guide to Literary Theory and Criticism* is available online to institutions or individuals. More ambitious is the *Major Authors* series produced by Primary Source Media. A longtime publisher of scholarly microform collections, Primary Source Media offers material typically available only in special collections: rare documents, manuscripts, and copyrighted material. The *Major Authors* series currently includes Whitman, Woolf, Cervantes, the Brontes, and Boswell/Johnson. Chadwyck-Healey, another publisher of online resources, offers annual subscriptions to *Literature Online,* a large collection of such massive databases as English poetry from Chaucer to 1900, English drama, early English prose fiction, and many others. Although much of this material is public domain, *Literature Online* also includes an impressive collection of reference materials (bibliographies, dictionaries, indexes, and so forth), links to other Internet sites, and, increasingly, more contemporary authors. Resources such as those sold by Primary Source Media and Chadwyck-Healey are usually encoded in SGML, fully searchable, updated regularly, and interactive. Electronic publishers typically offer flexible pricing, making their resources affordable to individuals as well as institutions, for classes as well as large libraries. Many prospective buyers may, however, pause before spending hundreds of dollars for a one-year subscription. Prices for libraries are also high, and libraries will have to make difficult decisions about where to spend their collection dollars. For the most part, printed books are a one-time expense for libraries, although some renewal is necessary, and subscriptions to periodicals and indexes are recurring costs. But annual payment for a complete electronic archive of Woolf or a complete database of English poetry puts new pressures on library budgets. Aware of this problem, some publishers plan to sell some of their databases in addition to offering subscriptions or license fees.

Some libraries are constructing massive digital versions of their own print collections. Since the libraries own the materials and do not need to pay annual subscription rates, they may be able to provide the resources free to all Internet users. The *American Memory* project, for example, offers focused collections—railroad maps, daguerreotypes, sheet music—compiled by the

National Digital Library Program, which is devoted to digitizing millions of documents held by the Library of Congress. Great Britain has assigned a portion of its national education budget to developing the *Arts and Humanities Data Service* (AHDS). It will become a national digital library that manages and provides access to a very large collection of digital resources, including the collection of literary texts in the *Oxford Text Archive*. The goal of AHDS, and similar services being developed by many state agencies in the United States, is to ensure uniform access to high-quality resources.

One of the most pressing issues as large-scale digital libraries are constructed is cataloging. All agree that standardization is essential, and Dublin Core is currently the most promising cataloging method. Dublin Core identifies fifteen elements—title, creator, subject, publisher, contributor, date, format, source, and so forth—that must be described. Acting like a title page or a card in a card catalog, this metadata (catalog data is the old-fashioned term) becomes a part of the electronic source itself, usually as a header at the beginning of the file. The hope is that Dublin Core will be used to catalog a wide variety, even all, of the digital materials a library collects. Librarians report that Dublin Core is uniform enough to be used for an entire library collection and for making many libraries searchable at the same time, and also that Dublin Core is flexible enough that libraries will be able to customize it to serve their own needs. As with markup codes and Internet technology in general, the goal of a universal cataloging system for digital collections is both standardization *and* specificity.

Finally, there is much speculation about the impact of digital resources on special collections. Some suggest that easy access to digital versions of rare books will help libraries to preserve fragile materials, but others believe that digitization will lead to much more consultation of the originals.

4. ACADEMIC CAREERS IN THE ELECTRONIC AGE

It is apparent that computers and the Internet will have some impact on academic careers in the humanities. Scholarship itself will surely change. The boundaries between lay readers and scholars may be blurred, and students and scholars may exchange ideas more readily as they visit each others' sites. Indeed, the division between teaching and scholarship may fade as sites are created that are both pedagogical and scholarly. Computer-assisted analysis will become more common as digitized texts are easily available. Sophisticated computer analysis has already proved to the satisfaction of most that a little-known Renaissance elegy was written by Shakespeare. User-friendly text-analysis software is also available, sometimes as shareware. For example, with Textual Analysis Computing Tools (TACT), a reader can work with an electronic text and produce a concordance, tag words for computer analysis, or discover stylistic or thematic patterns. Students and other readers are also using even simpler computing capabilities to do word searches and word counts as a way to comb a text or corpus for particular passages. Inevitably, new interpretations and methods will gain credence. Indeed, the very conversion of literary texts into electronic forms requires a preparation and manipulation of the text in logical and formal ways that prompt new approaches and discoveries.

The Internet will change academic publishing. Most academic publishers now use the Internet to promote and sell their books. Some academic presses allow Internet access to first chapters as part of their advertising efforts, and some books now appear simultaneously in print and electronic forms. These tactics, coupled with the ease of electronic sales of scholarly monographs at publishing sites and virtual bookstores such as *Amazon.com,* may improve sales and thus rescue academic publishing from the collapse some have predicted. Journal publishing will also change. Electronic journals may be revitalized as publishers promote a journal by publishing a table of contents, an article, an issue, or a few abstracts on the Internet. Some wonder if print journals will survive as publishers sell subscriptions to current issues or full archives of past issues to institutions or to individuals. Some peer-reviewed scholarly electronic journals are also available. *Early Modern Literary Studies, Postmodern Culture,* and *Romanticism on the Net* offer their journals on the Internet for no fee at all, *Critical Inquiry* publishes only its table of contents, and *Project Muse* sells subscription to all the journals published by Johns Hopkins University Press. Self-publishing is also common on the Internet. Some scholars publish works in progress, whereas others publish their teaching materials. Some scholars link full scholarly essays to their academic home pages, whereas others publish extensive electronic projects, using the hypertext environment and their own expertise to make important scholarly contributions. Some of these sites, after initially being freely available on the Internet, may then be acquired by a publisher. Populists lament the entrance of publishers and their fees into Internet publishing, but pragmatists suggest that the money and expertise that publishers can contribute to a project allow the project to use more advanced and expensive technology.

The Internet will change academic careers and fields. Some worry that publishing a dissertation on the Internet will limit print publication options later for the project and thus will handicap young scholars when they come up for tenure or promotion. Others celebrate what they believe will be a freer exchange of ideas, suggesting that electronic publication should be granted the same respect as print publication. These professional questions as well as the larger theoretical implications of the introduction of computers into literary studies are now commonly addressed at conferences and by those in the new field of Humanities Computing. Not yet fully institutionalized, Humanities Computing is concerned with how we use computers to study and teach literature and the arts and with the impact computers have on scholarship and knowledge. One of its greatest proponents, Willard McCarty, defines Humanities Computing as an academic field that focuses "both on the pragmatic issues of how computing assists scholarship and teaching in the disciplines and on the theoretical problems of shift in perspective brought about by computing" (McCarty, 1998). McCarty and others insist that those who specialize in Humanities Computing should not work in computer centers, which exist to maintain network infrastructure and provide services. Instead, McCarty envisions interdisciplinary programs in which scholars with traditional disciplinary affiliations and computer expertise teach and work both in their own fields and in the new field of Humanities Computing. Such programs would, presumably, help bring validity, time, and money to high-level scholarly computer projects. There are already a few such programs, such as the Humanities Advanced Technology and Information Institute at the University of Glasgow and the Institute for Advanced Technology in the Humanities at the University of Virginia. Schools that do not have separate programs are developing expertise in Humanities Computing by hiring scholars who are expert in literature and in computers and by supporting intensive, long-term computing projects. The increased interest in Humanities Computing is also evident in the appearance of such journals as *Computers and the Humanities* and *Literary and Linguistic Computing* and the electronic discussion list *Humanist.*

CHAPTER 9

Literature and the Internet: Theoretical and Political Considerations

INTRODUCTION

If electronic text on the Internet offers something radically different from the world of print texts, it does so on the basis of just three distinctive features, each described at length in earlier chapters of this book:

1. Its *searchability*. Hypertext on the Internet is much more searchable than the print texts in a physical library, within individual documents and web sites, and across the whole Internet.
2. Its *links*. Links within documents and between documents and sites make connections to any amount of supplementary and related text.
3. Its *accessibility*. For writers, the Internet offers a form of self-publication that bypasses the commercial constraints, distribution limitations, time delays, and other vetting and filtering processes of traditional print publishing. For readers, the Internet offers convenient, and often inexpensive, access to an unprecedented range of familiar and new kinds of material.

Considered individually, each of these features might be experienced mostly as an enhancement of traditional information technologies rather than as a revolution. We are used to searching libraries with catalogs, indexes, and bibliographies. Academic writing has always "linked" itself to other work by formally describing its relationship to other work in its field and through its footnotes and bibliographies. The new accessibility of the Internet is similarly a change of degree, not a change of kind. Not surprisingly, then, the Internet is often used in the service of quite traditional approaches to literary study. Material that was in the library is now also on the Internet. Primary and secondary materials are conveniently linked according to notions of the relationship between a literary text and its author or between a text and its historical context that the field of literary studies has been developing for decades. In combination, however, the basic tools of Internet navigation seem to promise—or threaten—much more than an extension of what we all have already been doing. Many commentators have suggested that we are in the early stages of a revolution as profound as that once initiated by the developments of movable type, the printing press, and a print culture. Arguably, we can anticipate changes in the ways we think as we move away from the "linear" and hierarchical arguments privileged by print technologies towards postmodern, "multivocal" networks of meaning. We might be facing radical revisions, or the complete destruction, of our sense of what counts as a text. The Internet might dramatically empower, or disempower, the reader. It might mean the death of the author, if she is not already dead, or it might give her a new kind of life. The Internet is a factor in our changing sense of geographical space. It will have political effects, perhaps as a force that helps revitalize democracy or perhaps as part of a tyrannical "globalization." The Internet is intellectually and economically productive, in its acceleration of the information age, or it undermines the legal and commercial institutions that have produced and disseminated quality information.

Some of this theorization or speculation about the Internet is futuristic and does not describe the ways we will read, work, and think in the next decade or so. Some of it will have few implications for literary study, but much of it is immediate and descriptive of the new things we can already do with the Internet and of the new ways it is already making us behave. This chapter presumes that information technology—the Internet in particular—is not simply a tool, but also an influence on our culture. It presumes that we should know what our new powers are and what we should defend ourselves against. After briefly describing some of the ways the Internet lends its technologies to familiar ways of reading and studying literature, the chapter surveys more problematic implications of the Internet for the text, the user, and the political world beyond them both.

1. THE INTERNET AND TRADITIONAL APPROACHES TO LITERATURE

Since its emergence at the beginning of the nineteenth century, the English curriculum has grown drastically. The canon has been greatly expanded and had little taken away from it, the discipline has been heavily theorized, and there is now a huge body of secondary writing. Indeed, Robert Scholes describes how there are these days so many approaches to literature, and so much secondary criticism, that "an enormous gap has become apparent between the ideal knowledge of the field and the actual knowledge attained by English majors, by graduate students, and even by faculty" (Scholes, 1998,

80). He identifies a problem that can potentially be addressed by hypertext on the Internet: The Internet can bring order and accessibility to a mass of literary and historical materials. At its most basic level, the Internet is an information technology, an invention that has arrived, fortuitously, when we need it most, to organize our culture. Once, a series of Norton Critical Editions could represent our canon and what we believed in doing with it. Now, our sense of canonicity is so exploded that no such series of scholarly editions could be produced to encompass it, and our varied approaches to literature could not be represented in a single volume. Computers' search capabilities are the new tool of information retrieval, and hypertext's links help arrange documents in relation to one another in the "post-Norton" literary field.

Although it is easy to herald hypertext and the Internet as postmodern, they often facilitate some of the most traditional scholarly projects. As George Landow notes, computer technology since the advent of word processing has helped the "old-fashioned job of traditional scholarly editing—the creation of reliable, supposedly authoritative texts from manuscripts or published books—at a time when the very notion of such single, unitary, univocal texts may be changing or disappearing" (Landow, 1997, 24). Equally, the capabilities of any search engine open any text called up on the Internet to kinds of analysis once only possible with laboriously and expensively produced concordances.

Hypertext links are a new technology, but they are most easily applied in the service of conventional conceptions of the relationship between a work and its author or cultural contexts. As J. Hillis Miller observes of Brown University's IRIS project in Victorian literature, "It presumes that a Victorian work like Tennyson's 'The Lady of Shalott' is to be understood by more or less traditional placement of the poem in its socio-economic and biographical context, by reference, for example, to the building of canals in England at the time" (Miller, 1995, 27). George Landow describes an undergraduate assignment to annotate an edition of Thomas Carlyle's "Hudson's Statue" on the World Wide Web, a traditional elucidation of text and context, intended to introduce students to the online versions of some equally traditional reference tools, such as the *Oxford English Dictionary* and *Encyclopaedia Brittanica*. Typically, the assignment produced the same kind of work that might have been done in print media, only at greater length: "[T]he absence of the same limitations upon scale that one encounters with physical editions . . . permitted much longer, more substantial notes than might seem suitable in a print edition" (Landow, 1997, 70).

To point out that these results of hypertext technology are conventional is not to be dismissive about them. Already, some Internet sites make available the kinds of material necessary for interdisciplinary approaches to literature that could once be only laboriously and expensively assembled. From the 1930s onward one appeal of "practical criticism" has been that it can be done with materials easily available to many ordinary readers; all one needed was a good poem and some knowledge of the stylistic techniques it was likely to be constructed with (see Eagleton, 1983, 45). Such explications—of poetry, especially—remain an exciting part of the classroom experience of literature; in just minutes of class discussion a poem that at first appears obscure can be brought to life by a teacher and some nonspecialist students. Other approaches to literature, however, are not as self-contained. The poem that can be first understood through its form also has historical, cultural, and political contexts that could illuminate it and its significance much further if only they were not inaccessible. Well-constructed sites like the *Victorian Web* and the *Wilfred Owen Multimedia Digital Archive* gather and link the resources readers, teachers, and students need for explorations of biographical, historical, and cultural studies approaches to literature, approaches that are not new but that hypertext makes newly practicable.

2. THE DEATH OF THE TEXT: REFIGURING WRITING

In the short term especially, the traditional approaches are likely to predominate on the Internet, given that most of the people who construct its sites went through graduate school without the new technology and their work thus reflects older ways of thinking about literature. As J. David Bolter points out, it has always taken many years for new technology to be utilized on its own terms: "Early printers tried to make their books identical to fine manuscripts: they used the same thick letter forms, the same ligatures and abbreviations, the same layout on the page. It took a few generations for printers to realize that their new technology made possible a different writing space, that the page could be more readable with thinner letters, fewer abbreviations, and less ink" (Bolter, 1990, 3). What appears new about the Internet may be only superficially so. The freedom of a user to control her own journey, for example, can be illusory: Links are placed according to the priorities of someone else, a site's authors, and they channel their user's experience much more than if she were browsing in a less directed way in a library.

On the other hand, even the above descriptions of traditional analytic or annotative practices may be seen to herald something distinctively new. Landow's undergraduates find a potentially radical freedom in the almost unlimited availability of Internet space. Their long annotations, and especially their extensive linking, are hailed by their teacher as examples of hypertext's reconfiguration of "the relative status of main text and subsidiary annotation" (Landow, 1997, 70). This question is not merely one of the relative space given to what in print could be distinguished as "primary" and "secondary" materials: "[R]eaders starting from Carlyle's text will experience linked materials on Chartism and the People's League as annotations to it, but readers starting with primary or secondary materials concerning these political movements will experience 'Hudson's Statue' as an annotation to them" (75). In fact, it becomes meaningless to talk in terms of primary and secondary sources at all.

The Internet is well named. It arranges itself—or, more precisely, does not arrange itself—as a net, or a web, of sections standing in multiple relation to one another rather than in straight lines of fixed sequences. There is no consistent place to begin an Internet inquiry, and after any beginning comes one of many possible paths chosen from many possible search results and subsequent links. Neither is there any conclusive end. There is thus no common text, even to readers pursuing similar inquiries. In an Internet world of hypertexts, what are the boundaries of the text? We are used to separating texts based on their production by a single named author, their binding as a single volume, or their definition by an essay or poem title. We are used to consuming texts individually. Our Internet experiences of hypertext are quite different. As we follow links, search and re-search, we cruise parts of documents and web pages. In an environment where part of a text is its links to other texts, there is, in an sense, no separability of texts at all, or there is only one huge text, of which we sample fragments.

As Landow and many others have theorized, there is a coincidence between these aspects of hypertext and recent poststructuralist critiques of "conceptual systems founded upon ideas of center, margin, hierarchy, and linearity" (Landow, 1997, 2). Hypertext is often described as the realization of a form that writers once could only dimly imagine, as the first chance to express what has for so long been repressed by the technology of print publication. In 1970, for example, Roland Barthes theorized a kind of writing freed of conventional forms, a "writerly text" in which the reader is "no longer a consumer, but a producer of the text" (Barthes, 1970, 4). Then, such texts were hard to imagine: "The writerly text is not a thing, we would have a hard time finding it in a bookstore." Today it is hard not to imagine them as the Internet:

> In this ideal text, the networks are many and interact, without any one of them being able to surpass the rest; this text is a galaxy of signifiers, not a structure of signifieds; it has no beginning; it is reversible; we gain access to it by several entrances, none of which can be authoritatively declared to be the main one. (Barthes, 1970, 5)

Like Barthes, Jacques Derrida sees the organizing principles of discourse that we live with every day as repressive, as having such a strong hold on us that we can barely think ourselves out of them. Unable to anticipate the Internet, he locates an alternative to present structures in an ancient suppressed "past of nonlinear writing," a time of "a writing that spells its symbols pluridimensionally; there the meaning is not subjected to successivity, to the order of a logical time, or to the irreversible temporality of sound" (Derrida, 1976, 85).

The case for the value of hypertextual prose made by J. David Bolter's *Writing Space* draws on such theorists and also gives examples of creative writing—Laurence Sterne's *Tristram Shandy* more than 200 years ago, Joyce, Borges—whose work has tried to exceed conventional forms. Landow argues similarly that Tennyson's "radically experimental" *In Memoriam* is an early striving for hypertextual form. Conventional narrative forms, read through from the first page to the last, force experience into a single line of development that real life might not provide. "Convinced that the thrust of elegiac narrative, which drives the reader and the mourner relentlessly from grief to consolation, falsified his own experiences," Tennyson created instead "an antilinear poetry of fragments" (Landow, 1997, 54). Today, the poem finds its appropriate technology, and perhaps also an appropriate literary criticism to help it along. Its heavily linked appearance on the *"In Memoriam" Web* can be seen as an enhancement of the poet's original project:

> The *"In Memoriam" Web* attempts to capture the multilinear organization of the poem by linking sections . . . which echo across the poem to one another. More important, using the capacities of hypertext, the web permits the reader to trace from section to section several dozen lietmotifs that thread through the poem. (Landow, 1997, 55)

Compared with this view of hypertext, printed articles and books can be made to appear restrictively or manipulatively linear. There is a genre of children's books that offers plots which are in part chosen by the reader. At a moment of crisis in the narrative (which is to say at the bottom of nearly every page) a decision—usually binary—is offered: "If you warn the aliens, turn to page 46. If you remain silent, turn to page 28" (Randall, 1985, 25). The story proceeds, in other words, through links. But these books exist mostly as novelties; they illustrate the limits of their form more than they do its possibilities, and usually the reader of an academic study is even less "empowered." An argument, or a small number of related arguments, probably set out as theses near the beginning, are made systematically and single-mindedly. For as long as the reader persists with the book she is almost completely subject to the voice of one author. She can take the argument or leave it, but not redirect it or reposition it amidst dissenting points of view.

Before we consider the innovations of hypertext form further, we should sound a cautionary note. We must be careful not to overstate the contrast between hypertext and print media. Although it is difficult to create hypertextual structure between the covers of a single piece of writing, each essay or book is in a sense a piece of a larger hypertext, a node in a larger network, comprehensible only in relation to other texts. Scholarly work usually takes care to situate itself in relation to other work in the field, to refer to other critics, and to primary sources. Any library, or even the endnotes and works cited at the end of an essay, is quite closely analagous to a hypertext system except that the referenced texts are spatially and temporally more distant. In addition, arguably literature, more than any other language, with its allusions, influences, and conventions, is ideally read as if it were hypertext anyway. When Scholes worked at Brown University in the 1970s on a humanities course that engaged a new system called hypertext, he says he "came to the conclusion that the most hypertextual items in the English curriculum were poems" (1998, 33). Miller describes Proust's *A la recherche du temps perdu* as "a huge database of memories. Marcel treats his memories as though he had a hypertext program for moving around within them" (1995, 37).

Landow recognizes the similarities between electronic hypertext and the links implied by all print writing and yet asserts that the new medium is "radically" different, changing "both the experience of reading and ultimately the nature of what is read" (1997, 4). He gives an example. If an article on James Joyce's *Ulysses* "was linked to all the other materials it cited, the article would exist as part of a much larger totality, which might count more than the individual document" (1997, 4). He might, however, be describing a difference of degree rather than a difference of kind. In a reader's mind the article probably does recede into a huge context of related and unrelated material soon after it is read. Similarly, when Bolter gives an example of nonlinear form, is he really describing something very new? He suggests for example that "[a] hypertext on the fall of the Roman Empire might include several explanations without seeking either to combine or reconcile them. Instead of confronting a single narrative, the reader would then move back and forth among several narratives, each embodying one of the explanations" (1990, 117). The way Bolter describes it here, however, there is nothing that could not be said, in conventional form, in a textbook survey of conflicting views of the fall of the Roman Empire.

These reservations aside, however, hypertext promises to bring about real revaluations of the form and status of the text. Often, the canonical literary text is described as suffering an erosion of a precious sanctity or aura. In its most reductive form, this is the complaint that hypertext on a computer screen is hard to read in bed. Miller laments that the downloaded version of Anthony Trollope's novel *Ayala's Angel* on his computer screen is not nearly as convenient or portable as his Oxford World's Classics paperback edition. The point he misses is that the Internet version is much easier to find than the print edition (last published in 1986 and now, according to *Amazon.com,* of uncertain availability) and in any case—precisely because reading it is uncomfortable—is unlikely to put the book out of print. There is also no reason for us not to anticipate, given a little more demand for them, new printing and binding formats that would make a downloaded book as portable and pleasurable as a prepackaged volume.

The classic text that appears on the Internet can be felt to undergo a revised

relationship to the world around it. Miller laments this as well. Even as he recognizes his own entanglement in our culture's "fetishism of the book" (1995,
28), Miller reacts to his beloved author's new association with "barbarous" file
names, "wierd" technical jargon, "garish" colors, and "strange" acronyms
(1995, 32). Poor Trollope is now caught in a "computer world [that] overlaps
with the world of popular music, the media, and such venerable expressions of
the counterculture as *Mad Magazine*" (1995, 32). Miller writes as if merely
naming these contexts is sufficient argument against them. Yet to complain that
"*Ayala's Angel* jostles side by side in cyberspace with weather maps, satellite
images, pornographic bulletin boards, the latest information about the human
genome project . . ." (1995, 32) seems to request an excessive insulation of literature from the rest of the world and to overlook that such contexts are always
present around a book: elsewhere in the bookstore, on the streets outside, and in
the reader's mind.

Undeniably, the technologies behind the Internet can change the experience of reading. Michael Camille's objections to computer screens are parallel to, but more sophisticated than Miller's. Camille argues eloquently that the
crucial "priority of sensation" in the experience of fully reading the "iconic
pages" of medieval manuscripts has become unavailable in their modern
electronic versions (1998, 33–34). He links consumption of medieval manuscripts on computer screens with a modern devaluation of all senses but the
visual, "the present reduction of reading signs to the purely ocular level"
(1998, 37). Medieval parchment books not only look glorious, they smell and
taste of their animal material origins, and they are experienced through touch
of the varied texture of their parchment or animal skin. "Opening a book to
see the pages was an act of intense sensational delight for the semiliterates as
well as literates and must have been part of a choric experience of seeing and
reading in groups" (1998, 38). The computer image, however, can only reproduce the "optical surface information from the original object" (1998, 37).
Yet even in this respect, Camille cautions, there are limitations. Current computer screens lack the definition and detail necessary to study the manuscript
"as a work of art" (1998, 45).

Camille concedes only that the virtue of Internet dissemination of manuscript is its accessibility. "Graphical user interface designs will make thousands of previously unavailable manuscript pages available in the home"
(1998, 45). Martha Nell Smith is much more positive, arguing, unlike
Camille, that hypertext reproductions can recapture qualities of manuscripts
that have been flattened by the restrictions of book publishing:

> Though displayed on a cool screen . . . samplers of electronic archives of
> [Emily] Dickinson materials . . . have repeatedly elicited audience re-
> sponses that testify to the near sensate experience of viewing photographic
> representations of the manuscripts in color and in close-up. Halftone repre-

sentation in books smothers many of the material signs, making strokes of the pen almost impossible to distinguish from strokes of the pencil and occluding a range of signs as all is flattened into shades of gray. The screen places readers in a virtual state quite different from, if intimately bound in relation to, the pages of a book. Screen images cannot be held, eaten, drunk, nor breathed, yet in their luminosity they do make the manuscript object more palpable to the imagination. Reader after reader has remarked how much more vibrant is the cartooning manuscript "A poor—torn Heart—a tattered heart" . . . on the screen, where Dickinson's flamboyant use of pink yarn to attach cutouts from Charles *Dickens's The Old Curiosity Shop* is on full display, rather than in the halftone, shades-of-gray reproductions I have previously used in books. (1998, 203)

On Smith's *Dickinson Electronic Archives* or sites like the *F. Scott Fitzgerald Centenary Home Page*—which is also packed with photographic reproductions of handwritten manuscript drafts, a family scrapbook, and other materials—a new technology unsettles the definitiveness of literature's print incarnations. Certainly we could ignore the many variant forms or at least continue to privilege the print-published versions as the best refinements of the writer's intentions. Or we can see the print texts as selections from a more expansive project, finished and fixed only by the demands of the publishing industry. As on a compact disc reissue of a classic jazz album that is filled out with bonus "alternate" takes, a familiar text is seen to exclude other possible creative directions. As Smith puts it, "hypermedia urges readers beyond the closures and certainties of print and beyond the possessiveness of definitude that would fix and settle the questions raised by such dynamic writing" (1998, 215).

Hypertext, like Barthes's writerly text, is not a material object, buyable in a bookstore. For Miller and Camille its intangibility would be the source of its falsity: "[t]he computer ends up being an extension of our wired brains rather than our tired bodies" (Camille, 1998, 45). For Smith and others, this is the secret of its malleable, expansive multiplicity. Its incorporeality may also produce a more literal loss of stability: there are real concerns that hypertext is not durable. Miller feels the fragility of the Trollope novel on his laptop when he notes that it "would disappear in an instant if the power failed" (1995, 30). More significantly, however, the electronic novel could easily be turned off at its source.

The durability of print text has over the centuries led to an accumulation of resources: primary and secondary sources in book form as well as millions of essays, articles, reviews, news reports, cartoons, illustrations, photographs, and advertisements in newspapers, magazines, and journals that now sit on the shelves of many libraries. These paper materials have survived not because they were always actively used or because anyone had a clear sense of their future value. Many of them have never been in any sense canonical; for decades or more they may have been disregarded and unneeded by academia's critical trends; they are kept as a matter of principle, for the historical record. Until their paper decomposes, they can remain on library shelves. It remains to be seen whether hypertext will have such longevity. For one thing, print materials often exist in multiple copies, in many places, whereas material on a website is likely to be maintained in only one place. Second, print materials often survive through inertia; it takes institutional effort to decide to discard them. It is the maintenance of a website, on the other hand, that takes institutional effort. Websites exist at the mercy of technological change or failure; the changing priorities or character of institutions; the interests, energies, retirement, or death of an individual maintaining a site. Over time they might be updated and revised, according to changing notions of what counts as relevant and important information, so that their past incarnations are discarded.

A single lapse of commitment can consign materials into permanent oblivion as it likely would not for materials on paper in a traditional library. We acknowledge this impermanence when we include the most recent date we used a website in our works cited listings; unlike with print media, we know that our readers may not long be able to access the same sources. Recently I found on the Internet a wonderful bibliography of Chartist literature and of course immediately converted it to old-fashioned, durable print form lest it be unavailable when I next need it. If this unreliability is so apparent in the short term, the long-term durability of hypertext must be highly questionable. It is often said that the Internet vastly increases access to all kinds of contemporary voices; it may also be forever purging itself of its past.

To see the transience of hypertext more positively, we might examine productive aspects of its perpetual revisability. Even after it is made public, hypertext does not have to be thought of as finished. What began to become true for the writing process in the early 1980s, when writers began to compose on word processors, can now apply also to published writing. Those of us who can remember the labor of revisions on typewritten manuscripts appreciate the impermanence of electronic text. But revisibility is generally halted by print publication; an academic writing project is likely to be part of professional considerations—writing books for tenure and promotion, for example—so that completion of the book enters it on the resume, ends the project, and licenses the beginning of a new interest. Only rarely is published work taken up again, for a second edition or for incorporation of a journal article into a book. Print publication thus postpones wide public exposure of research until it is sufficiently "finished" and then abruptly curtails the writing process at that point. Internet publication, however, promises an extension of the revisable text comparable to that introduced by word processing in the 1980s. Writing *always* has only draft status, so projects might as well be published earlier and, perhaps more importantly, can be developed indefinitely. One's involvement with a hypertext research project is not halted; it can be put aside, but taken up later, or it can be expanded and linked to other work.

Finally, the Internet encourages publication of material that does not fit the forms of established print technologies, but which is nevertheless valuable. Bolter predicts that "[e]lectronic writing will probably be aphoristic rather than periodic" (1990, ix), which is not to say unrigorously shapeless. Rather, smaller units of thought will link to each other, in isolation from a single extended argument. Until recently, the publications of a literary critic were likely limited to a journal essay or a book. Now that it has become possible to bypass the many stages of print publishing, however, she can publicize a wider range of materials. On the Internet, teachers, critics, students have posted course syllabi and descriptions, teaching notes, and many kinds of works in progress. Richard Cornwall's home page on queer theory and teaching <www.middlebury.edu/~cornwall> is one of thousands of examples. The site contains abstracts of essays on queer studies, syllabi and other materials for three queer studies courses, illustrations, and poetry. What might be posted primarily for the use of students in a college class also has currency for others. Any and all work that makes it into writing can be published. The Internet thus begins to redefine the kinds of information that have public value and to deliver alternatives to the kinds of linear argument we are used to buying from print publishers.

3. THE BIRTH OF THE USER: REFIGURING THE READER

The reader of hypertext, first of all, is not merely a reader: he is a *user.* His new title perhaps suggests a promotion or an empowerment. As the authority of the text diminishes, the power of the user increases in ways that are usually theorized as positive, but that can also be regretted. Miller makes an almost moral issue of the new empowerment when he coins the phrase "the ethics of hypertext" in describing the necessity for readers to take "responsibility" for their routes through the Internet:

> A hypertext . . . offers the reader the necessity at every turn of choosing which path to follow through the text, or of letting chance choose for him or her. Nor is there any "right" choice, that is, one justified objectively, by a preexisting meaning. A hypertext demands that we choose at every turn and take responsibility for our choices. This is the ethics of hypertext. . . . The reader, in the end, is responsible for what he or she makes of a text. (1995, 38)

Again, Barthes is a key figure in theorization of a writerly text, which is to say a text within which a reader can be active and creative. We are all familiar with arguments about the brain-deadening passivity of television viewing. Barthes, unlike most critics of television, would apparently refuse to see literature as much of an alternative:

> The reader is . . . plunged into a kind of idleness—he is intransitive; he is, in short, *serious;* instead of functioning himself, instead of gaining access to the magic of the signifier, to the pleasure of writing, he is left with no more than the poor freedom either to accept or reject the text: reading is nothing more than a *referendum.* (1974, 4; emphases in original)

As the reader navigates hypertext, however, he makes decisions about where to go, what links to follow, and where to center and recenter the network. He creates his own text, not only accepting and rejecting, but shaping.

In practice, the control offered by links can be offset by uncertainty about what or where a link leads. Like a superscript endnote number in a print text, the mere hotlinking of a word or phrase gives little clue to the information at the other end. The experience of pursuing an unsatisfying link and then backing out of it is in fact not unlike that of fumbling for the page at the back of a book that has the right endnote and then disgustedly looking for where one had read to before the distraction. It is difficult to navigate the Internet when you cannot see where you are going. E. Jeffrey Conklin calls this the "disorientation problem": "Along with the power of being able to organize information much more complexly comes the problem of having to know (1) where you are in the network and (2) how to get to some other place that you know (or think) exists in the network" (quoted in Landow, 1997, 115). It is technologically possible to label links, which allows for a brief "previewing" of their content, but such labels are in practice rare.

A system of self-navigation through links can also pose a threat to directed learning. In reading an old-fashioned book, it is precisely the subjection or commitment of the reader to the structure or argument of a single expert author that is productive. From this perspective, empowerment of the reader to pick and choose what she reads might be seen as empowerment of the uninitiated, of someone who needs a guide, who would benefit from a willing suspension of her freedom. Is a system where the user chooses her own pathways a system for exposure to new ideas or for confirmation of what already feels comfortable? When we think of reading and researching as simple information gathering, this problem is less apparent. When, however, we consider the value of a constructed argument put together by specialists—say, the massively researched study by William Bowen and Derek Bok (1998) on the effects of affirmative action in higher education—the whole point might be that it has taken years of labor, and much expertise, to draw conclusions from fragmentary information.

Equally, however, links might be said to provide just the right amount of direction for active learning. Although a mass of contextual materials for literature is available in any decent college library, that context is in practice unavailable to many readers not primarily because of physical retrieval difficulties, but because beginners in a field are unaware of what kinds of context count or are worth pursuing. Landow describes the difference between an expert and a neophyte reading of a literary text. Whereas the former, perhaps a professor expert in a specialized field, would experience a poem extensively "situated within a field of relations and connections, her student encounters a far barer, less connected, reduced poem, most of whose allusions go unrecognized and almost all of whose challenges pass by unperceived" (1997, 280). Traditional annotated editions, where they are available, go some way to making up this shortfall, but almost never to the extent possible through hypertext linking. On the Internet, too, are not only the polished final products of academic research that students are used to seeing as models for their own writing, but also other kinds of writing that expose professionals' ways of thinking, debating, negotiating, and hypothesizing. Electronic discussion lists, for example, publicize the passion of arguments about what might seem to outsiders to be small points, but that are important to specialists. Exchanges on listservs are likely to reveal riskier, broader thinking than would be committed to print and will sometimes be more colorful and more topical, illustrating the significance of historical and literary points by relating them to modern controversies.

Further, time spent pursuing links can be instructive not only about a particular literary text, but about the kinds of connections that are productive in literary and cultural studies in general. There is some theory and research to suggest that because reading in hypertext is more active than reading a book, learning is more thorough. Even the "disorientation problem" can be productive here, as a difficulty that drives readers into active learning, to reading with the necessity of a kind of attentiveness and mastery that produces long-term retention and the ability to use, rather than simply memorize, information. Students have access, through the Internet, to the viewing and the practice of a world of research and debate that they once could only gaze at from outside.

4. THE END OF GEOGRAPHY: REFIGURING THE WORLD

Just as the Internet can revise our sense of the text and of the reader, it threatens to reform also the academic, national, and even global environments in which literature is studied. Peter Lyman is concerned that new technologies will not support the "marketplace of ideas" currently founded on "three institutions—libraries, publishing, and copyright law" (1996, 1). In Lyman's view, our society has up until now developed a well-functioning balance between commercial incentives to the production of knowledge—that is, the profits of writing and publishing, which are protected by the idea of intellectual property—and accessibility, maintained by free access to publications in libraries. "Libraries in America are situated on the boundary between the market and the polity, in a liminal space that provides free access to knowledge in order to fulfill the public interest in education and democratic participation" (1996, 2). Lyman argues that the commercial side of print publishing is necessary for the maintenance of quality information. Drawing on a book by Carla Hesse, *Publishing and Cultural Politics in Revolutionary Paris, 1789–1810,* he cites the "egalitarian" abolition of copyright during the French Revolution, which backfired by reducing the quality of published works. Similarly, "the Internet may well fail as a public institution because it is entirely a gift culture and therefore suffers from poor-quality information" (Lyman, 1996, 28).

Academic publishing, of course, often is not motivated by financial rewards, and it is hard to imagine that much academically sponsored literary criticism would go unproduced because it might be given away free on the Internet. The bulk of the labor of writing a book or article is not directly rewarded in the current print publishing system, and all that is needed to completely bypass print publishers is some minimal skills and labor and some technology that is widely available in academic settings. In addition, the Internet, of course, does not have to be entirely a gift culture. It is already as easy to subscribe to hypertext journals as to print journals or to pay to download a work as to buy a book. As Lyman explains, however, the simple mechanisms of commercial Internet publication complicate the idea of the public library. The concept of a digital library, a central repository of commercially produced works, with free public access, analogous to current public libraries full of print materials, would completely undermine any possibility for a publisher to sell a work in any other way. With current print publishing, library materials are available to me but not as conveniently as if I owned them; there remains incentive to buy books. But why would I pay to get something from one site if it was free from another site?

Lyman argues eloquently that "[p]ublic access to knowledge is of fundamental importance in a society where access to learning is subsidized in order to support a theory of social justice, which emphasizes equality of opportunity in the economy and democratic participation in the polity" (1996, 23). But his is not the only view of this matter, as his qualified description of social justice as a "theory" perhaps suggests. The current commercial system of publishing can be seen as exclusionary and elitist to the extent that circumventing it would be preferable. James Boyle, for example, argues that copyright law, which grants ownership to ideas as if they were material property, inhibits the public interest. "Copyright is a fence to keep the public out" (Boyle, 1996, 18), and when the public domain is limited, ideas are restricted from speedy circulation and use. The Internet can challenge our assumptions about the materiality of publishing and thus our sense of how to define copyright. In fact, computer-based communications technologies already deliver a productive subversion of copyright. E-mails, or listservs among groups of scholars, for instance, function a little like journals, but at much higher speeds and without much legal regulation. Bolter describes how, when subscribers to a listserv type excerpts from books or articles into their communications without need to think about copyright, "[t]he notion of copyright seems faintly absurd, since their messages are copied and relayed automatically hundreds of times in a matter of hours" (1990, 29).

The writing of academics, which is generally not financially motivated, might be more economically and more widely disseminated on the Internet. One reason this situation does not widely occur, however, is the reliance of academic institutions on the publishing system for its tenure and promotion evaluations. A book placed with a prestigious publisher is better than a book with a lesser publisher is better than no book at all. The feasibility of Internet publication challenges these evaluation criteria and highlights their unreliability. The politics of publication are surely an imperfect way to value a researcher's contribution to her field—even academic publishers are concerned with sales—yet they substitute for more independent evaluation. It is likely that the pressure towards Internet publication will require English and other departments to sponsor independent evaluations of research themselves and to build their reputations for faculty status in other ways.

As the Internet blurs the boundaries of institutions within a nation, it also assaults international distinctions. We are living, it is often said, in an age of increasing "globalization," and the Internet might be the new world's ideal information technology. The theory of globalization sees the significance of national borders diminishing under the influence of such developments as the end of the Cold War and the fall of European communism, the spread of capitalism and Western-style democracy, the increasing power of multinational corporations, and the influence of international trade agreements and of organizations like the United Nations, the World Bank, the International Monetary Fund, and the European Community. Brian Langille (1998) adds to this economic and political globalization the idea of an equally significant "globalization of the mind," an increasingly hegemonic discourse of rights and values largely exported from the West.

Publishing institutions have always played a part in the definition and maintenance of national boundaries. Over the past few centuries, the organizing principle of print publication has tended to be the individual nation-state. Local laws regulate the speech that can be physically distributed in a geographical area, national libraries are the definitive repositories of information, and print technologies have produced works that tend to be distributed mostly within the boundaries of a single nation. The Internet, clearly, exceeds conventional borders and is all but unregulable by any government's information policies. Groups or political movements that might once have been censored, marginalized, or denied access to print and other media by their uncommercial nature now have a much less regulated voice. Organizations whose interests transcend national boundaries—such as international labor organizations, Amnesty International, or environmental groups like Greenpeace—can already use the Internet's global reach. Miller links new communication technologies with a transformation of the university, as he anticipates "the replacement of the Humboldtian university in the service of a single-nation state by a new technologized transnational university that serves the global economy" (1995, 27).

As always, we should be careful not to exaggerate such predictions. The consumption of international literature is always inhibited by language barriers. The academic disciplines of literary studies in English-speaking countries, conducted by scholars who almost always read and write only in English, and where the international distribution of texts—between, say, England and the United States—is already fairly widespread will probably not be thoroughly transformed by the Internet's globalism. There are, however, imaginable real effects. Critical perspectives originating from outside the English-speaking world do have an influence—as when, for example, French poststructuralist philosophy and theory filtered into English departments in the 1980s—and this might happen more rapidly when international criticism is available on every critic's desktop computer. It is also imaginable that Miller's vision of education's transcendence of geography will be furthered by the Internet's, and e-mail's, potential for distance learning.

Cultural globalization can easily be viewed negatively. The freer dissemination of information can in practice amount to a modern form of colonialism; like freedom of trade, it can mean freedom within the terms established by the United States and other western economies. According to this view, the influence of marginal voices on the new global culture is far outweighed by the power of those who have the technology to dominate, that is, the United States. Rather than exchanging culture, the rest of the world gets what we put out and absorbs that in place of its indigenous culture. The Internet will have an influence on the world's intellectual culture analogous to that of Hollywood on international film culture.

On the other hand, the Internet can be celebrated as an opportunity for marginalized voices. Landow, like many others, argues that "the history of information technology from writing to hypertext reveals an increasing democratization or dissemination of power" (1997, 277). Writing exteriorizes memory and disseminates knowledge; print publication was a huge advance on handwritten manuscripts, and the Internet represents a comparable leap. Lyman draws a comparison to the advent of libraries: "[h]istorically, the great public libraries have been public spaces serving immigrants and minorities" (1996, 19). The Internet similarly increases the accessibility of information.

At one obvious economic level, this point is arguable, given the cost of Internet access and of an adequate computer system. Until the Internet is in every home, it is only exacerbating existing divisions between the information haves and have-nots. Yet it might at least be said that in the affluent environment of college-level literary studies this new democratization is more real.

The Internet dissemination of alternative voices is a force, for example, in revision of the literary canon. Despite recent attacks on the exclusivity of the traditional canon—which is seen to lack diversity of gender, race, class, nation, aesthetic values, and so on—efforts to expand it can be hindered in part by publishers' commercial interests. No matter how much it is revised, for practical purposes the canon will cohere around the books that are affordably available. Thus, the literary canon has been perpetuated by such institutions as the anthology, a drastically limiting consensus about the most valuable works. The Internet challenges the power of the anthology by offering its own storehouse of works, already one of massive proportions. Not only can teachers assign students to read works on the Internet, but they can easily construct their own anthologies of public domain materials by downloading and printing them. These anthologies are revisable from one term to the next, according to a teacher's developing sense of what students need, what works in her classroom, or her current interests and expertise.

It is thus easy to see the Internet as a democratic technology. Henry Giroux distinguishes between modernist and postmodernist notions of democracy, and his description of the latter concept fits well with some of the boundary- and hierarchy-breaking tendencies of the Internet. For Giroux, old-fashioned, modernist political liberalism is rooted in Enlightenment ideals of democracy that have been progressive, but that are now ripe for expansion. Postmodernism, on the other hand, offers the regenerative energy of "a general attempt to transgress the borders sealed by modernism, to proclaim the arbitrariness of all boundaries, and to call attention to the sphere of culture as a shifting social and historical construction" (Giroux, 1994, 18). As we have seen above, for example, the Internet's circumvention of commercial print publishing delivers something more radical than expansion of the canon; potentially it could lead to the abolition of the notion of canon altogether.

Like Giroux and many other post-Marxist critics, Dick Hebdige has defended postmodernism as a source of productively oppositional critical thinking:

> If postmodernism means . . . the opening up to critical discourse of lines of enquiry which were formerly prohibited, of evidence which was previously inadmissible so that new and different questions can be asked and new and other voices can begin asking them; if it means the opening up of institutional and discursive spaces within which more fluid and plural social and

sexual identities may develop; if it means the erosion of triangular forma-
tions of power and knowledge with the expert at the apex and the "masses"
at the base; if, in a word, it enhances our collective (and democratic) sense
of *possibility,* then I for one am a postmodernist. (1989, 226)

He writes in 1989, well before the practical advent of the Internet, but the
connections are obvious. The Internet has been seen to collapse traditional
definitions of the text and to open up the narrow orderings of experience required by linear narrative forms. Classic literature on the Internet finds itself
unsettled by its lack of materiality and its new contexts; without a canon, it
finds itself no longer classic. The Internet gives access to new voices and sub-
verts conventional definitions of intellectual property. Whether or not it will
one day usher in a revitalized democracy, the Internet is a powerful force that
can reasonably be characterized as postmodern. We accept that in the remark-
ably few years it has been widespread, it is changing our daily lives. Every
day, the media carry stories of the Internet phenomenon: the rivalry between
Amazon.com and Barnes and Noble and the effects of their growth on physical bookstores, changes to the ways we shop in general, Internet pornography
and censorship, chatrooms, hacking and fraud, digital broadcasting, and the
Internet in the classroom, to name a few. For those in academia, it will also
change intellectual life, offering new ways of seeing and, perhaps, inhibiting
some of the old ones. The more we are conscious of its power, the better we
can use it and resist it.

Works Cited

Barthes, Roland. *S/Z.* 1970. Trans. Richard Miller. New York: Hill and Wang, 1974.

Bolter, J. David. *Writing Space: The Computer in the History of Literacy.* Hillsdale, NJ: Erlbaum, 1990.

Bornstein, George, and Theresa Tinkle, eds. *The Iconic Page in Manuscript, Print, and Digital Culture.* Ann Arbor: University of Michigan, 1998.

Bowen, William G., and Derek Bok. *The Shape of the River: Long-Term Consequences of Considering Race in College and University Admissions.* Princeton: Princeton University Press, 1998.

Boyle, James. *Shamans, Software, and Spleens: Law and the Construction of the Information Society.* Cambridge: Harvard University Press, 1996.

Camille, Michael. "Sensations of the Page: Imaging Technologies and Medieval Illuminated Manuscripts." In Bornstein and Tinkle, 33–53.

Derrida, Jacques. *Of Grammatology.* 1967. Trans. Gayatri Chakravorty Spivak. Baltimore: Johns Hopkins University Press, 1976.

Eagleton, Terry. *Literary Theory: An Introduction.* Minneapolis: University of Minnesota Press, 1983.

Gates, Joanna E. "Literature in Electronic Format: The Traditional English and American Canon." *Choice* 34, 8 (April 1997): 1279–96.

Giroux, Henry A. "Rethinking the Boundaries of Educational Discourse: Modernism, Postmodernism, and Feminism." In Kostas Myrsiades and Linda S. Myrsiades, eds., *Margins in the Classroom: Teaching Literature.* Minneapolis: University of Minnesota Press, 1994. 1–15.

Hebdige, Dick. *Hiding in the Light.* New York: Routledge, 1989.

Hockey, Susan. "Evaluating Electronic Texts in the Humanities." *Library Trends* 42, 4 (Spring 1994): 676–93.

Landow, George P. *Hypertext 2.0: The Convergence of Contemporary Critical Theory and Technology.* Baltimore: Johns Hopkins University Press, 1997.

Langille, Brian. Presentation. World Conference on the Universal Declaration of Human Rights. International Civil Aviation Organization, Montreal. 8 December 1998.

Lavagnino, John. "Completeness and Adequacy in Text Encoding." In Richard J. Finnenan, ed., *The Literary Text in the Digital Age.* Ann Arbor: University of Michigan Press, 1996. 63–76.

Lyman, Peter. "What Is a Digital Library? Technology, Intellectual Property, and the Public Interest." *Daedalus* 125, 4 (Fall 1996): 1–33.

McCarty, Willard. "What Is Humanities Computing? Toward a Definition of the Field." 19 May 1998. <http://ilex.cc.kcl.ac.uk/wlm/essays/what/>. 15 January 1999.

McMillan, Gloria. "Playing Dracula Tag: The Adventures of the Two-Housewife *Dracula* TEI-tagging Team." *Humanist.* 11.0049 (20 May 1997). <http://lists.village.virginia.edu/lists_archives/ Humanist/v11/0049.html>. 15 January 1999.

Miller, J. Hillis. "The Ethics of Hypertext." *diacritics* 25, 3 (Fall 1995): 27–39.

Pitti, Daniel, and John Unsworth. "After the Fall—Structured Data at IATH." Presented at 1998 ALLC/ACH Conference, Debrecen, Hungary. <http:www.iath.virginia.edu/ ~jmu2m/ach98.html>. 15 January 1999.

Randall, E. T. *Thieves from Space.* Mahwah, NJ: Troll, 1985.

Ryan, Michael. *Marxism and Deconstruction: A Critical Articulation.* Baltimore: Johns Hopkins University Press, 1982.

Scholes, Robert. *The Rise and Fall of English: Reconstructing English as a Discipline.* New Haven: Yale University Press, 1998.

Shillingsburg, Peter L. and D. C. Greatham. *Scholarly Editing in the Computer Age,* 3rd ed. Ann Arbor: University of Michigan Press, 1996.

Simon, Leslie D. "Present at the Creation." *Wilson Quarterly* (Autumn 1998): 39–40.

Smith, Jonathan. "What's All This Hype About Hypertext?: Teaching Literature with George Landow's *The Dickens Web.*" *Computers and the Humanities* 30 (1996): 121–29.

Smith, Martha Nell. "Corporealizations of Dickinson and Interpretive Machines." In George Bornstein and Theresa Tinkle, eds., *The Iconic Page in Manuscript, Print, and Digital Culture.* Ann Arbor: University of Michigan Press, 1998. 195–221.

Stauffer, Andrew M. "Tagging the Rosetti Archive: Methodologies and Praxis." *Journal of Electronic Publishing.* December 1998. <http://www.press.umich/edu/jep/04-02/stauffer. html>. 15 January 1999.

Index

Learning Resources
Centre